KIDSPORTS

A Survival Guide for Parents

Nathan J. Smith   Ronald E. Smith   Frank L. Smoll

Addison-Wesley Publishing Company
Reading, Massachusetts   Menlo Park, California   London
Amsterdam   Don Mills, Ontario   Sydney

Copyright © 1983 by Nathan J. Smith, Ronald E. Smith, and Frank L. Smoll

Library of Congress Cataloging in Publication Data

Smith, Nathan J., 1921–
  Kidsports, a survival guide for parents.

  1. Sports for children.   2. Parent and child.
I. Smith, Ronald E.   II. Smoll, Frank L.   III. Title.
GV709.2.S53 1983   796'.01'922 83-10000
ISBN 0-201-07826-0
ISBN 0-201-07827-9 (pbk.)

Cover photograph by Marshall Henrichs
Text design by Janis Capone
Set in 11 point Goudy Old Style
by Jay's Publishers Services, Inc.

ABCDEFGHIJ-DO-86543
First printing, August 1983

To parents, children, and families,
and their growth through sports

Acknowledgments

We wish to acknowledge gratefully the contributions of three colleagues. The tables and conditioning schedules in Chapter 5 were developed by Dr. William L. Haskell, Co-Director of Cardiac Rehabilitation, Stanford Medical School. They originally appeared in *Handbook for the Young Athlete* (Palo Alto, Calif.: Bull Publishing Company, 1978). Dr. Vern Seefeldt, Director of the Youth Sports Institute at Michigan State University, allowed us to reprint information and quotations from *Spotlight on Youth Sports,* a newsletter for coaches (pages 8, 9, 14, 15, 17, 20, 174, 175, 214). And Dr. Rainer Martens, Director of the Office of Youth Sports at the University of Illinois, granted permission to include materials from *Sportsline* (pages 8, 12, 22, 213, 214, 215).

Nathan J. Smith
Ronald E. Smith
Frank L. Smoll

Contents

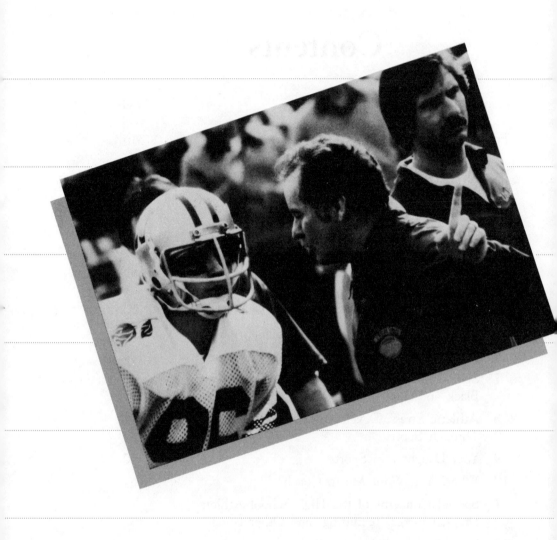

Foreword

Sports touch nearly every family, and often they originate in a youth program.

Although I am a college football coach, I have had two children participate in youth sports programs, and a third is participating now. I regret not having had an opportunity to read *Kidsports* before they became involved.

Youngsters entering sports for the first time usually are participating for the enjoyment and camaraderie of being with their friends. But when my children started in youth sports, I can remember being extremely upset with the attitudes and conduct of parents toward officials, coaches, and even their own youngsters.

There is a tendency among parents to become children's severest critics, when in most cases what a young athlete needs is a pat on the back, not criticism.

Kidsports offers suggestions on what role parents should assume from the time their youngster starts youth sports through recruitment by college coaches.

It offers suggestions not only to the parents of gifted athletes but also to parents who have youngsters of average athletic ability and to coaches who will have to deal with a variety of athletes and their parents. It also provides helpful information on proper diet and exercise for young athletes.

Although only a small percentage of young athletes will be recruited by colleges and universities, for those who are and for their parents, it can be a very trying and emotional period. It is a time when proper input from parents can help a young athlete through a very stressful period and help him or her make a correct decision on which university to attend.

Athletics can be a very enjoyable experience for parents and athletes, or they can become a source of tension and frayed nerves for both. *Kidsports* provides information and guidelines for decision making that can help make youth sports what they should be — an enjoyable and enriching experience for both.

Don James
Parent and head football coach,
University of Washington
1977 College Football Coach of the Year

KIDSPORTS

1

You and Your Child in Sports

Sanity and Madness in Competition

Dear Mom and Dad:

I hope you won't get mad at me for writing this letter, but you've always told me to tell you if anything was bothering me. This has been on my mind for a while, but I haven't been able to get myself to talk about it.

Remember the other night when my team was playing and you were sitting and watching? Well, I hope you won't get mad at me, but you kind of embarrassed me. Remember when I struck out with the bases loaded? I felt really bad about that, but even worse when I heard you yelling at the umpire. Actually, the pitch was a strike, but that pitcher is so fast I just couldn't swing. Then later in the game when the coach took me out in the fourth inning so Danny could play, I really feel bad that you got down on him, because he's trying to do a good job. He really loves baseball and loves coaching us kids.

Dad, I know you want me to be a good ball player like you were, and I really do try as hard as I can. But I guess I just can't measure up to what you want me to be. The way you act when I don't do good, it makes me feel like I've let you down. On the way home the other night, neither of you spoke to me. I guess you were pretty sore at me for messing up. You made me feel like I never wanted to play baseball again.

Even though I'm not very good, I love to play and it's lots of fun being with the other kids. But it seems like the only time you're happy is when I do really good — even though you told me that playing sports was supposed to be for fun and to learn the game. I want to have fun, but you keep taking the fun away. I didn't know you were going to get so upset because I couldn't become a star.

This is really hard to say, and that's why I have to write it to you. I used to be really happy that you came to our games. Some of the kids' parents never show up. But maybe it would be better if you stopped coming so I wouldn't have to worry about disappointing you.

Love,
Chris

Chris's letter leaves little doubt that his parents are having a real impact on his youth sport experience. Unfortunately, it is not the kind of impact that one would wish for him. Perhaps Chris's parents are lucky, for their son has the courage to give them feedback on something that is bothering him deeply and influencing his enjoyment of sports. Maybe they can change their behavior, realizing how they are unintentionally becoming a source of stress rather than a source of support. Like all parents, they want the best for their child, and they may honestly feel that they are supporting him in his sport activities. It also seems clear, however, that there needs to be a change in their attitudes and behavior if the sport experience is to bring Chris and his parents closer together and to contribute to his enjoyment of the activity. Parents can be a source of support or they can create stress for young athletes.

This book is for you, the parent of the young athlete. We are writing it because we believe that participation in sports has great potential for enhancing the growth and personal development of children and for family enrichment. Because sports are so important to children, what parents do and say in relation to the sport experience can have an important long-term impact on the child. We hope that this book will provide parents with information that will help make the sport experience constructive and enjoyable. All parents do as well as they can, given the limits of their awareness. It is hoped that the medical and psychological information in these pages will increase your awareness and help you to deal more effectively with the many problems and opportunities that can arise in youth sports. We recognize an opportunity to increase the knowledge of parents who have a strong background in sports as well as those who have had little exposure to them.

The Growth of Youth Sports

How big are youth sports and how did they get that way? Although their growth has been phenomenal over the past thirty-five years, organized youth sports in the United States actually go back to the early 1900s. The first programs were instituted in public schools when it was recognized that physical activity was an important part of education. Over time, sponsorship and control of some sports have shifted to a host of local and national youth agencies. Little League Baseball is one of the oldest of these. It originated in 1939 in Williamsport, Pennsylvania, as a three-team league for eight- to twelve-year-old boys. The program was so popular that it spread rapidly. By 1949, more than 300 Little Leagues (comprised of mostly four teams) were operating in eleven states. Today there are some 14,000 chartered leagues in twenty-nine countries and territorial possessions around the world. Their enrollment includes more than 2.5 million boys and girls six to eighteen years of age.

Programs for other sports also showed rapid growth, and now more than 25 million children between the ages of six and sixteen participate in nonschool athletic programs in the United States and

Canada alone. A recent and highly significant development has been the growth of sports programs for girls and young women. More than six times as many females participate in organized sport programs today as in 1975.

Growth of the sports movement has demanded the involvement of increasing numbers of adults. Nearly 2.5 million men and women volunteer their time as coaches, league administrators, and officials. As programs become more highly organized, parental involvement, of necessity, must increase.

The youth sport explosion has touched boys, girls, and adults in increasing numbers. Several factors have contributed to the rise of organized youth sports. Over the years there has been a clear recognition of the importance of wholesome leisure-time activities for children. Furthermore, the mushrooming of large cities has decreased the amount and availability of play spaces for spontaneous, self-generated play. Many authorities have looked to sport programs as a way of reducing juvenile delinquency. Finally, sport has become an increasingly central part of our culture as we have become more fitness-minded and as the mass media have brought sporting events into the homes of virtually every family. But even these factors would not be sufficient to account for the growth of youth sports if it was not for the fact that sports are an enjoyable and rewarding pastime. The most important reason why people participate in sports is that sports can and should provide fun and enjoyment.

The growth in the scope of youth sports and in the role that they play in the lives of children is undeniable. But this expansion has generated persisting and at times bitter debate. Thoughtful persons have raised questions about the desirability of organized sports for children, and the answers to their questions are not simple.

Organized Youth Sports: The Debate Lingers On

We have already summarized some of the reasons for the rapid growth of youth sports. Obviously this growth could not have occurred if it was not believed that participating in organized sports is beneficial. Those who favor sports programs emphasize that there are many aspects of the experience that contribute to personal development. Some have pointed out that sport is a miniature life situation in which children can learn to confront and cope with many of the important realities of life. Within sport, children learn to cooperate with others, to compete, to deal with success and failure, to learn self-control, and to take risks. Important attitudes are formed about achievement, authority, and persistence in the face of difficulty.

Adult leadership is viewed by many as one of the truly positive features of organized sports programs. Knowledgeable coaches can help children acquire physical skills and begin to master a sport. Higher levels of physical fitness can be promoted by such guidance. More than just a teacher, the coach becomes a significant adult in the life of the child and can have a profoundly positive influence on personal and social development. Likewise, the involvement of parents can bring families closer together and heighten the value of the experience for young athletes.

But youth sports have more than their share of critics. Attacks on sports programs abound in the popular media. Because abuses involving children are newsworthy, sports abuses are likely to be sensationalized and widely publicized. Distortions seem to occur readily. One prominent sport psychologist recently spent ninety minutes with a reporter. For eighty minutes he discussed the positive aspects of sports programs, and for ten minutes he talked about the problems in youth sports. The newspaper article dealt only with the problems and misquoted the expert as saying that all organized sports should be eliminated for children under the age of sixteen. The media's overemphasis on the negative has understandably made some parents question the value of youth sports.

Undoubtedly problems can arise in sports programs, and some of these problems have been the focus of severe criticism. *Newsweek* once published a thoughtful editorial by former major league pitcher Robin Roberts, entitled "Strike Out Little League." This Hall of Fame baseball star charged that Little League Baseball can place excessive physical and psychological strains on youngsters and that programs sometimes exist more for the self-serving needs of adults than for the welfare of children. Experts in child development have charged that adult-supervised and highly organized programs can deprive children of the creative benefits of spontaneous play. They suggest that children would benefit far more if adults simply left them alone to their own games and activities.

Many complaints center around the role of adults in youth sport programs. Critics have charged that some coaches are absorbed in living out their own fantasies of building sport dynasties and that consequently they show little personal concern for their players. Likewise, opponents of youth sports maintain that parents live through their children's accomplishments and place tremendous pressure on them to succeed. When coaches and parents become more focused on themselves than on the quality of the experience for children, something is undoubtedly wrong. The negative involvement of adults in sports has been linked to such problems as inappropriate use of drugs for training and conditioning purposes, physical injury due to excessive training and competition, and blatant cheating and dishonesty. Not long ago, the *Los Angeles Times* reported that an ignorant and misguided coach injected oranges with amphetamines, then fed them to his ten- to twelve-year-old football players to get them "up" for a game. The *Washington Post* carried a story about a mother who forged a phony birth certificate for her seventeen-year-old son so that he could star in a league for fourteen-year-olds.

Who's right? Are youth sports a symptom of a serious, pervasive social disease? Or are they the saving grace of our youth? The answer is neither. No reasonable person can deny that important problems do exist in some programs. Some of the criticisms are well founded and can be constructive. On the other hand, surveys have shown that the vast majority of adults and children involved in sports find them to be an enjoyable and valued part of their lives. Sports programs are what we make of them. They can become a source of joy and fulfillment in the life of a child, or they can become a source of stress and disappointment.

We believe that sports have a strong positive potential for achieving important objectives. The question is not whether youth sports should continue to exist; they are here to stay as a firmly established part of our society. If anything they will continue to grow in spite of the criticisms that are sometimes leveled at them. The real question is how parents can help ensure that sports will be positive for their children. What can we as adults do to help achieve the many desirable outcomes that are possible? Perhaps the key to unlocking the potential of youth sports lies in being well informed of their physical and psychological dimensions. It is hoped that the information presented in this book will serve you well in your role as successful sport parents.

The Rights of Child Athletes

When children enter a sports program, they automatically assume responsibilities. But they also have rights. Adults need to respect these rights if children are to have a safe and rewarding sports experience. The National Association for Sport and Physical Education's Youth Sports Task Force has developed a "Bill of Rights for Young Athletes." The rights identified by these medical experts, sports scientists, and national youth sport officials are represented in the following box.

Bill of Rights
for Young Athletes

1. Right to participate in sports
2. Right to participate at a level commensurate with each child's maturity and ability
3. Right to have qualified adult leadership
4. Right to play as a child and not as an adult
5. Right to share in the leadership and decision-making of sport participation
6. Right to participate in safe and healthy environments
7. Right to proper preparation for participation in sports
8. Right to an equal opportunity to strive for success
9. Right to be treated with dignity
10. Right to have fun in sports

We believe that the "Bill of Rights" provides a sound framework for fulfilling adult responsibilities toward young athletes. These rights will be dealt with in greater detail throughout the book as we explore their implications for enriching the sport experience.

Goals and Models in Youth Sports

What do you want your child to get out of sports? What are the goals and objectives that you would like achieved? Your parental goals can range from simply wanting to get the child out of your hair for a few hours to wanting your child to become an Olympic champion or professional athlete. Of course, there are many other goals that may well be more appropriate. Some of them are physical, such as attaining sports skills and increasing physical fitness. Others are psychological, such as developing leadership skills, strong identities, sportsmanship, competitiveness, cooperativeness, self-confidence, and other positive attributes that fall under the heading of "character." Many parents agree with Dallas Cowboy coach Tom Landry that "the greatest contribution that sports can make to young athletes is to build character. The greatest teacher of character is on the athletic field." Youth sports are also an important social activity in which children make new friends and acquaintances and become part of an ever-expanding social network.

Whatever your objectives may be, it is important that you become aware of them and realize that none of these objectives is certain to be attained merely through participation. Simply placing a child into a sport situation does not guarantee a positive outcome. The nature and quality of the program, which are very much dependent on the input of adults, are prime factors in determining benefits.

The major goals of professional sports are directly linked to their status in the entertainment industry. Former Dallas Cowboy wide receiver Peter Gent recalled that at the end of rookie camp, a meeting was held to explain the responsibilities of a professional athlete. "The man to give the best advice was the team's public relations director," Gent said. "He told us, 'Boys, this is show business.'"

The goals of professional sports, simply stated, are to entertain, to win, and to make money. The measure of success or failure resides in the won-lost column and in the financial receipts. In the professional sports world, players are commodities to be bought, sold, and traded. Their value is based on how much they contribute to winning and profit-making. They are the instruments of success on the field and at the box office, and they are dealt with as property or as cogs in a machine. Professional athletes are often glorified by the media to create an image intended to draw paying customers and generate interest in the team. However, many professional athletes feel that little real concern is shown them as human beings or contributing members of society. For example, several professional teams have reportedly turned deaf ears to reports of drug abuse by star players as long as the players continue to perform well. Following his trade to the New York Mets after a long and illustrious career with the New York–San Francisco Giants, Willie Mays tearfully remarked that "all they seem to care about is what you did for them yesterday and what you can do for them tomorrow." More recently, basketball star Bill Walton charged the Portland Trail Blazers with injecting him with pain-killing drugs so that he could perform in a crucial playoff series. He claimed that this led to injuries that placed his career in jeopardy.

The professional coach's job is to win. Those who don't usually join the ranks of the unemployed rather quickly and unceremoni-ously. No gold watches for years of service, either! A win-at-all-costs philosophy is required for advancement and, indeed, survival. Professional coaches do not receive bonuses for developing character. Their primary function is to help the franchise to compete successfully for the entertainment dollar.

The developmental model of sports has a far different focus. As its name suggests, the goal is to develop the individual and to provide an enjoyable recreational experience. The most important product is the quality of the experience for the child. In this sense sports participation is an educational process, during which valued skills and personal characteristics are acquired. Although winning is sought after, it is by no means the primary goal. Profit is measured not in terms of dollars and cents, but rather in terms of the personal benefits that the young athlete derives from sports.

We are firmly convinced that most of the problems in youth sports occur when adults erroneously impose a professional objec-tive on what should be a recreational and educational pursuit. When excessive emphasis is placed on winning, it is easy to lose sight of the needs and interest of the young athletes.

We asked earlier what you want your child to get out of sports. Perhaps we also should ask children what *they* want from sports and why *they* wish to participate. This has been done in several studies in the United States and Canada. These carefully conducted scientific surveys indicate that young athletes most often participate in organized sports for the following reasons:

- To have fun
- To improve their skills and learn new skills
- To be with their friends or make new friends
- For thrills and excitement

- To become physically fit
- To succeed or win

It is important to note that the primary goals of the professional—succeeding or winning—are far less important to children. Their primary goals are to have fun, to learn skills, and to be with friends. In one of our own studies, we found that teams' won-lost records have nothing to do with how well young athletes liked the coaches they played for or with their desire to play for the same coach again. Interestingly, however, success of the team was related to how much the children thought their parents liked the coach. The children also felt that the won-lost record influenced how much their coach liked them. It appears that at a very young age, children begin to tune in to the adult emphasis on winning, even though they do not yet share it themselves. *What children do share in common is a desire to have fun.*

Fun. A term we use a lot. But what is it? Certainly it's easy to tell when people are having fun. They show it in their expression of happiness, satisfaction, and enthusiasm. We've asked many children why sports are fun for them. Perhaps the most basic reason was given by a little eight-year-old girl, who said, "Fun is when I'm doing something that makes me happy just to be doing it, like tennis." In other words, much of the fun in sports comes just from performing the activities themselves. One child played on a soccer team that almost never won matches. Yet the youngster could hardly wait for the coming season. Why? Because she had fun. She simply enjoyed being with others and playing soccer. Being with others, meeting challenges, feeling the drama of uncertain outcomes, becoming more skilled, all of these add to the fun of doing for doing's sake. Winning also adds to the fun, but we sell sports short if we insist that winning is the most important ingredient. In fact, several studies reported that when children were asked where they'd rather be—warming the bench on a winning team or playing regularly on a losing team—about 90 percent of the children chose the losing team. The message is clear: the enjoyment of playing is more important to children than the satisfaction of winning.

We adults cannot allow ourselves to neglect the basic right of the child athlete to have fun in participating. One of the quickest ways to reduce fun is to begin treating children as if they were varsity or professional athletes. Speaking to a group of parents and coaches, major league baseball manager Sparky Anderson warned, "It's a disgrace what we're doing in the United States and Canada. We're asking kids to compete to win. Why not ask them to compete to have fun? We're trying to build our own egos on little children."

Perhaps most importantly, we need to keep in mind that young athletes are not miniature adults. They are children and they have the right to play as children. In fact, we all do. The Dutch philosopher Johan Huizinga wrote that to play as an adult, everyone must become a child again. Youth sports are first and foremost a play activity, and children deserve to enjoy sports in their own way.

Now, we are not suggesting changing the team names or taking away the uniforms. The youngsters enjoy these trappings. What we are stressing is the need to make sure that our programs remain child-centered and do not become adult-centered.

A Winning Philosophy for Youth Sports

Vince Lombardi was a winner. During his years as coach of the Green Bay Packers, he created a professional football dynasty the likes of which had never been seen before. His team was the scourge of the NFL during the 1960s, a team driven to near perfection by an intensely competitive, perfectionistic leader. The image that Lombardi conveyed was perhaps captured best in his famous statement, "Winning isn't everything, it's the only thing."

If you are a sports fan or perhaps even if you are not, you have heard Lombardi's famous quote. But did you know that Lombardi never actually said that? Years after his death, it was revealed by Lombardi's son that his father had been misquoted. What Lombardi actually said was, "Winning isn't everything, but striving to win is."

John Wooden was another winner, and so were the UCLA Bruins who played for him. During a twelve-year period from 1963 through 1975, his teams won the national collegiate basketball championship ten times. Certainly, to be that successful Wooden and his Bruins had to be single-mindedly focused on winning games. And yet, at least where Wooden was concerned, this seems not to have been the case. In fact, what he did communicate to his teams may be the key to their success and their ability to play well under pressure. John Wooden once told an audience of parents and youth coaches:

> You cannot find a player who ever played for me at UCLA that can tell you that he ever heard me mention "winning" a basketball game. He might say I inferred a little here and there, but I never mentioned winning. Yet the last thing that I told my players just prior to tip-off, before we would go on the floor, was, "When the game is over, I want your head up, and I know of only one way for your head to be up. That's for you to know that you did your best. No one can do more . . . You made that effort."

Yes, Lombardi and Wooden were winners. Their won-lost records speak for themselves. Yet it is interesting to note that both coaches placed an emphasis on the process of striving for excellence. Their vision went beyond a preoccupation with winning games. Instead, they demanded that their players dedicate themselves to 100 percent effort.

The conventional notion in sports equates success with victory: scoring more points, runs, or goals than the opponent. This notion of success emphasizes records and objective standards. Winners win and losers lose—everyone knows that. Yet we suggest that the measure of a person's or a team's success goes beyond records and standings. Success is a personal thing and is related to one's own standards and abilities. John Wooden captured this relationship when he offered the following definition of success: "Success is peace of mind, which is a direct result of self-satisfaction in knowing you did your best to become the best that you are capable of becoming."

In our mind, Wooden's perspective on success may be the most important reason why he deserves the title Wizard of Westwood. He realized that everyone can be a success, because success relates to the effort that one puts into attaining one's potential.

It is important that adults involved in youth sports teach children that success does not require winning games and that losing does not mean one is a failure. Rather, the most important kind of success resides in striving to win and in giving maximum effort. We need to realize that the only thing our children (or any of us) have complete control over is the amount of effort we give. We have very incomplete control over the outcome that is achieved. If adults emphasize the value of competitive effort, which

Winners ... on Winning

The purpose of organized youth sports programs should be to teach the child how to play the sport, about competition, about winning and losing, and about playing on a team. And the emphasis should be on the individual going out and enjoying what he is doing. Every game will have a winner and loser. The only successful youth sports program is the one with a coach who will accept the losing along with the winning, last place in the league along with the first place, and still be able to congratulate his team for their efforts.

Roger Staubach,
former Dallas Cowboy quarterback

There are many things a young athlete can learn in sports, but unless fun, as well as discipline, practice, heart, and desire, makes up a huge part of the game, I do not believe one will develop into the total athlete. You hear of many great sports figures giving up their careers because the fun had left the game. A winning desire should be stressed at all levels, but it shouldn't be a life-and-death situation. Simply give your best and have fun doing it.

Gordie Howe,
professional hockey player

Competitive stress is directly related to the emphasis placed on the child by the adult coach or manager. The object of youth sports is the spirit of competition and the development of sportsmanship. Adult emphasis on the child to win must be tempered by the belief that competitive effort combined with a sense of fair play will help to alleviate added stress.

Steve Garvey,
professional baseball player

Players should not get too high after a success or too low after a failure. You have to keep things in perspective. I've learned that when you lose, the sun still comes up in the morning, and when you win, time doesn't stand still. You always look ahead.

Matt Bahr,
professional football player

Competitive sport is pursuing perfection in a self-chosen movement task. It's trying to reach 100 percent of one's potential and being satisfied with nothing less. For those who make such an effort, perfection is possible — momentarily possible, but nevertheless attainable. The feeling, the high experienced from achieving each of these moments of perfection, is why people play.

Competition between players is nothing more than two people pushing and helping each other to be more than they can be alone. Few people in our society can look back over their lifetimes and say that they were the very best they could possibly be at one self-chosen task. The sport competitor can.

Dr. Donna Lopiano, *director,*
women's intercollegiate athletics

The bottom line in youth sports competition should not be based on the pressure to win. Instead, it should be on the enjoyment of competing and the opportunity to develop positive attitudes toward other people through that competition.

Lute Olson,
college basketball coach

the child can control, and downplay the importance of winning, over which the child has limited control, an important source of pressure is lifted from the child's shoulders.

If we can impress upon our children that they are never losers if they give maximum effort, we are giving them a priceless gift that will assist them in many of life's endeavors. A volunteer soccer coach had the right idea when he told his team, "You kids are never losers when you try your best, but sometimes the other team will score more goals."

Does this mean that children should not try to win? Definitely not! As a form of competition, sport involves a contest between opposing individuals or teams. It would be naïve to believe that winning is not an important objective in sports. To play sports without striving to win is to be a dishonest competitor. But despite this fact, it is important that we not define success only as winning. Not every child can play on a championship team or become a champion athlete. Yet every child can experience the true success that comes from trying his or her best to win. The opportunity to strive for success is the right of every young athlete.

As we stated earlier, one of the great virtues of sport is that it is a miniature life situation in which many valuable lessons can be learned. Children can learn both from winning and from losing. In fact, some of the most valuable lessons can be learned from losing. Children can learn to persevere in the face of obstacles and to support one another even when they do not emerge victorious. They can also learn that mistakes are not totally negative, but are important stepping stones to achievement. Mistakes provide valuable information that is necessary for improving performance. Thomas Edison was once asked whether he was discouraged by the failure of more than three thousand experiments leading to the development of the light bulb. Edison replied that he did not consider the experiments failures, for they had taught him three thousand ways not to create a light bulb and each experiment had brought him closer to his goal.

Parent Roles and Responsibilities

Two important sets of adults combine with the child to form the athletic triangle. They are, of course, parents and coaches. The relationships that exist among the points of the athletic triangle go a long way toward determining the quality of experience the child has in sports programs. Being a point in the athletic triangle implies both rights and responsibilities.

When your child enters a program, you automatically take on some obligations and responsibilities. Some parents do not realize this at first and are surprised to find what is expected of them. Others who never realize their responsibilities miss opportunities to help their children grow through sports, or they may actually do things that interfere with their children's development. In a sense this entire book is about parents' roles and responsibilities. For now, however, we want to summarize some of the more obvious ones.

The right of the child to participate in sports also implies the right not to participate. Although parents might choose to encourage participation, children should not be pressured, intimidated, or bribed into playing. If youngsters feel forced or pushed, it decreases their chances of having that enjoyable experience — fun. It can have even more profound and long-lasting effects on your relationship with your child. An extreme and very sad example of this is the following statement made to one of us by a New York executive: "If it hadn't been for sports, I wouldn't have grown up hating my father." It is possible to be very supportive of a child's athletic interests without placing demands or pressures on the youngster. For example, hockey great Bobby Orr was fortunate in having very supportive parents.

He recalls, "My parents bought my equipment, drove me to the rink, rubbed my feet when they were cold. I can't ever remember them saying that I was going to be a professional hockey player."

"Parents should be observers and supporters of their athletically inclined children, but never pushers," Johnny Majors, a college football coach, once advised. Although coaches have the most direct contact with children within the sport environment, parents also involve themselves to varying degrees. Some parents assume an extremely active role, and sometimes their behavior and the demands they place upon children become a great source of stress for the child. Consider, for example, the following experience described by a youth coach:

> One night last season my team lost a close game. I sat the whole team on the bench and congratulated them for trying, for acting like gentlemen. I said I couldn't have been prouder of them if they had won. Most of all, I said, it is as important to be a good loser as a gracious winner. As I talked I could see their spirits lifting. I felt they had learned more than just how to play baseball that night. But as I mingled with the parents in the stands afterward, I was shocked to hear what they were saying to the boys. The invariable theme was, "Well, what happened to *you* tonight?" One father pulled out a note pad and went over his son's mistakes play by play. Another father dressed down his son for striking out twice. In five minutes the parents had undermined every principle I had set forth.

It is natural for parents to identify with their children to some extent, to take pleasure in their triumphs, and to suffer in their defeats and disappointments. The love bond that exists between parent and child virtually guarantees this process. Like all good things, however, this process of identification can become so excessive that the child becomes an extension of the parent. When this happens parents may begin to define their own success and self-worth in terms of how successful their child is, as in the following cases.

Tommy's father never was a good athlete. Now in his adult years, he is a "frustrated jock" who tries to experience through Tommy the success he never knew as an athlete. Tommy is pushed to excel, to put in long hours of practice, and to give up other activities. When he performs poorly, his father becomes withdrawn and gloomy. Dad takes home movies of Tommy during practices and games, and visitors to the home are promptly shown some of Tommy's triumphs. Tommy himself is a reasonably good athlete at age twelve, but he is unlikely ever to become a superstar. In fact, a school teacher has become very concerned because Tommy "doesn't seem himself" and is lagging in his schoolwork. The family's physician is concerned even more, because Tommy has been complaining of abdominal pains and the doctor is fearful he may be developing an ulcer.

Sheila's mother was a champion collegiate swimmer who won a bronze medal in the Olympic Games. It is clear that the mother expects Sheila to follow in her footsteps. Sheila was a "waterbaby" at six months of age and was "in training" by age four. She shows every sign of becoming a high-level competitor in her own right. She is now ten years of age and has won countless medals in age-group swim competitions. Her mother clearly is delighted with and totally engrossed in her athletic development. But her father is becoming worried. Lately, Sheila doesn't seem to enjoy swimming as much. Last week she announced that she wanted to stop training and go to summer camp with some friends for several weeks. Her mother flatly refused to consider this, and Sheila burst into tears, saying that she didn't want to swim anymore. Sheila's father is concerned that her mother is placing so much pressure on the child to excel that she is experiencing burnout.

Tommy and Sheila are showing clear signs of the stress caused when parents try to live through their children. Tommy is being pushed to become the great athlete that his father always wanted to be, and Sheila is having to measure up to the standards set by her mother as a champion athlete. These children must succeed or their parents' self-image is threatened and the children themselves are threatened with disapproval or loss of love. Much more is at stake than a mere game or swim meet, and the child of such a parent carries a heavy burden.

At some level both Tommy and Sheila must be aware that their parents' happiness depends upon how well they perform. Children are accustomed to being dependent on their parents and are often unequipped to handle a reversal of the dependency relationship.

This is especially the case when the parent is demanding winning *results* rather than the best effort of which the child is capable.

We should point out that sports are not the only realm of activity in which this may occur. The performance arena may be in academics, music, dance, or social popularity—any activity that has social or personal importance for the parent. But because of the importance of sports in our society, and particularly in the world of many parents, there is special potential for the dependency-reversal process to occur in the realm of sports.

One of the most important aspects and responsibilities of child-rearing is the role that parents play in shaping their children's perceptions and understanding of their world. Sports can be a proving ground for later life experiences. Therefore, you have the opportunity to help your young athlete accurately interpret and understand sport experiences and place them in a proper and healthy perspective. For example, you can play a key role in helping your child understand the significance of winning and losing, of success and failure. You can help your child define his or her success in terms of effort expended instead of the score at the end of the contest. Moreover, winning or losing a contest may be the result of external factors beyond the child's control, such as officials, weather, other players, or luck. Or it may be the result of internal causes, such as the child's ability and effort. By helping children to accurately interpret the causes of outcomes of sport events, parents help youngsters view the world more realistically.

There are other important challenges that must be met by the parent of the child athlete. First, you will need to decide how much time you are willing and able to commit to your child's activity. It may involve driving children to and from practice, going to your child's games or matches, and assisting the coach. Many parents do not realize how much time can be consumed by such activities. Some parents who expect sports programs to occupy their child's time and give them more time for themselves are shocked to find that they are now spending more time with their children than before. Conflicts arise when parents are very busy, yet are also interested and want to encourage their children. Thus, one challenge is to deal honestly with the time-commitment issue and not to promise more than you can actually deliver.

Every child athlete experiences "the thrill of victory and the agony of defeat" as part of the competition process. You will be called upon to accept your child's triumphs and to support your child when he or she is disappointed and hurt. Accepting a child's triumphs sounds easy, but it is not always so. Some parents may feel competitive with their children, a process that is the opposite of the overidentification discussed earlier. For example, when Jack played well in a basketball game, his father pointed out minor mistakes, described how other players did even better, and then reminded his son of even more impressive sport achievements of his own, reestablishing his role as a dominant parent and thoroughly deflating Jack.

Disappointments are also part of sport and they may be keenly experienced by your child at times. Would you be embarrassed if your child broke into tears after a tough loss or after making a mistake? Could you put your arms around and comfort your child at such a moment? Can you tolerate becoming a target for your child's displaced anger and frustration when there is no other outlet for disappointment and hurt? One of your most positive contributions can be to change your child's disappointment into self-acceptance. Again, emphasizing effort rather than outcome can be an important means to this goal.

Conduct at practices and during games can have an important impact on your child. Parents who yell at or criticize players, coaches, or officials set an incredibly poor example for their youngsters. You are a significant role model for your child in all aspects of life, including sport. It is not surprising to find that parents who exhibit poor self-control in their own lives often have children who are prone to emotional outbursts and poor self-discipline. If we are to expect sportsmanship and self-control of our children, we need to exhibit the same qualities in our own behavior. Professional football coach Sam Rutigliano impressed this responsibility on parents with the following poem:

> A careful man I want to be,
> A little fellow follows me.
> I do not dare to go astray
> For fear he'll go the selfsame way.

One of the opportunities that sport provides is the chance for children to acquire and practice adult behaviors. An essential part of growing up is accepting responsibility for one's own behavior and decisions. The latter can become a real challenge to parents, for once you invite the child to make his or her own decisions, you need to support and live with those decisions. As a child matures, you should provide encouragement, suggestions, and guidance about sports. But ultimately, within reasonable limits, parents need to let their children become more independent and self-reliant. For example, making commitments to a team or program is an important decision, as is a decision to quit a team. At times such as these, parents must accept that they cannot control their children's lives. Decisions about sports can offer parents an introduction to the major process of letting go and allowing their children to become adults in their own right.

A final challenge relates to the third point in the athletic triangle, your child's coach or manager: Can you give up your child to another significant adult? Many issues can arise in your relationship with the coach, including the way in which he or she is coaching the team or relating to your child. You are putting your youngster in the charge of another adult and trusting him or her to guide the sport experience. Beyond that, you must deal with the fact that the coach may gain admiration and affection that was once yours alone. It is natural for a coach to become a very important figure in a child's life at a time when a tendency toward independence is causing the child to move away somewhat from parents. One father described his difficulty in adjusting to his child's coach:

> I was used to being number one in Mark's life. I was the man he looked up to, the man with all the answers, the man he wanted to be like someday. Things began to change a bit when he joined the basketball league. He was placed on a team run by the most popular coach in the league, a man who had played college ball and who has a real charisma with kids. All of a sudden, all we heard at the dinner table was, "Coach said this and Coach did that." It became more and more clear that my son had a new hero, and one whom I couldn't compete with. I've thought about it a lot and I can understand that what's happening is perfectly normal, but it's not easy to take a back seat in my child's life, even temporarily.

When parents cannot accept the entry into the child's world of a new and important adult, youngsters may suddenly find themselves in the middle of a conflict between parent and coach in which the child is subtly pressured to make a choice between the two. Like allowing your child more freedom to make more decisions, sharing him or her temporarily with another esteemed adult (and one toward whom greater esteem seems to be shown at times) can be an important part of the process of letting go.

Sport offers your child many opportunities for personal growth and development. It also offers parent and child opportunities to interact in ways that enrich their relationship. It is our hope that this book will contribute to a better understanding of you and your child in sport.

A Child's Plea

Well, here it is another hockey season,
So I am writing you for just one reason,
Please don't scream or curse and yell,
Remember I'm not in the N.H.L.
I am only 11 years old
And can't be bought or traded or sold,
I just want to have fun and play the game
And am not looking for hockey fame
Please, don't make me feel I've committed a sin
Just because my team didn't win
I don't want to be that great, you see
I'd rather play and just be me
And so, in closing, I'd like to give you one tip —
Remember, the name of the game is
SPORTSMANSHIP.

Donny Chabot, age eleven
Sault Sainte Marie, Ontario

2

The Psychology of the
Young Athlete

Mind and Motives

The development of a human being is a truly remarkable process. In only nine months two microscopic cells change into a fully formed human infant. Six years later the newborn has become a walking, talking first-grader ready to master such complex skills as reading, arithmetic, relating to others, and sports. From here, a process of rapid mental, physical, and social development advances the child into the storms and challenges of adolescence and then into such adult roles as worker, husband or wife, and parent.

As parents, we have a window to the wonders of growth and development in our children. We are surprised, chagrined, gladdened, and saddened as we observe and participate in this passage through the years of childhood. We are excited by rapid events of evolving maturity. And at the same time, we are saddened by the realization that we and our children can never recapture the delights of earlier ages, now preserved only in our photo albums, home movies, and hearts.

The concept of childhood as a separate stage of development has existed only since the seventeenth or eighteenth century. Prior to that time, children were simply phased into the adult world at about age seven, when they began to work alongside their elders. Childhood as we know it today emerged partly as a result of the Industrial Revolution, when large numbers of people entered the middle class, leisure time increased, and infant mortality decreased. Families became less dependent on child labor for economic survival, and with more children surviving the ravages of disease, parents could allow themselves to become more emotionally invested in their children. Meanwhile, the development of formal schools separated children from the rigors of the adult world, and new education theories focused on the child's mental, social, and moral development. Children found new freedom to play, to experiment with social roles, and to learn needed skills.

In three centuries we have thus moved from an era in which childhood was unrecognized to one in which we protect it with numerous legal, social, and educational institutions. Their collective effect has delayed children's entry into adult status until late adolescence. Adolescence, an even newer concept, is now seen as a complex transition period, during which a person moves from childhood into adulthood.

As childhood became established as a separate and crucial period of development, the functions of play attracted the attention of educators, medical doctors, and scientists. To understand the role of sports in the life of the child, we must first consider the meaning and functions of play itself.

Play and the Developing Child

Animals as well as humans engage in play activities. In animals play has long been seen as a way of learning and rehearsing behaviors that are necessary for future survival. For example, baby lions stalk and pounce on objects in their play. In children, too, play has important functions during development.

From its earliest beginnings in infancy, play is a way in which children learn about the world and their place in it. Much of the first two years of life are spent learning about objects and events. By handling and manipulating objects in the environment, infants gain information about how to respond to the world and how it responds to them.

Between the ages of two and seven, the child spends most of his or her waking hours involved in imaginative and other kinds of play. In their play children take on a variety of imaginary roles. With time they become responsive to playmates and begin to understand the effects of their actions on them. The parallel play of toddlers, who simply play side by side, evolves into cooperative play with others. Play now becomes an important avenue for social development. Children can try out various kinds of social interactions by creating rules for games or by developing ways to cooperate, share, or compete. They can experiment with different roles and actions, and they can sample the consequences without actually experiencing the dangers that the real action might hold. Johnny can play the bad guy and experience the punishment only indirectly. Through make-believe play, children can test skills — such as driving a car or cooking a meal — that they might not be allowed to try in reality at that time. Children's play can thus serve as an apprenticeship for later life.

Play provides a wonderful means of learning through imitation. By observing the actions of others and the results that occur from them, children learn skills and gain information about their world. A television superhero can provide a model of courage, generosity, and helping. Children can also learn new skills, such as building with blocks or mastering an electronic video game, by watching more skillful peers.

In later childhood, play changes from the dramatic fantasy of the young child to games regulated by rules that everyone accepts. Beyond age six, children spend a great deal of time making up exact rules, and they place strong pressure on one another to follow them. Through this process children learn that social systems are cemented together by rules and that the good of the group demands the individual's willingness to abide by the rules. This is the beginning of consideration for the rights of others.

Play helps children learn about their world and serves as a training ground for skill development. Play also continues to serve as a training ground for social behaviors and personality characteristics that will be important in adulthood. Children's games allow them to acquire mental, social, and physical skills. Decision-making skills are refined in games such as checkers and chess, and physical skills in games such as soccer and baseball. Children learn to compete, too, but within a safe world where the consequences of losing are minimized. Younger children often attach little significance to who wins or loses. In contrast to adults, they often get their enjoyment from experiencing, not just from winning.

During the early elementary school years, the world of the child broadens dramatically to include not only the family and playmates but a widening circle of schoolmates and adults. In this expanded environment children discover and judge their own abilities and begin to form a stable self-concept and feelings of self-worth. Academic and social experiences provide important information, as do the reactions of peers and adults in the child's life. It is during this critical period of development — the years between six and twelve — that most children enter organized-sports programs. This is why sports experiences can play such an important role in children's personal and social development.

Sports and Self-Concept Development

Self-concept consists of views and beliefs about ourselves. It includes our perceptions of personal traits and abilities, particularly those that are important in shaping our identities as distinct people. *Self-esteem* refers to the way we feel about our own characteristics —

as good or bad, valuable or worthless, and so on. Our self-concept and self-esteem are of central importance in how we function in the world. They underlie our view of who we are, what we are capable of, and how we can expect others to react to us.

None of us was born with a self-concept. It began to develop as we entered our world. As children mature, they gain more and more information from their experiences. Two types of information are particularly important with regard to self-concept and self-esteem development. The first is how significant people in their lives respond to them. From such reactions children draw conclusions concerning how other people feel about or evaluate them. Children often have little more than the reactions of others to go on. It is no wonder that such information has such a strong influence on the formation of their sense of who they are and how worthwhile they are. Thus, a child who consistently receives attention, approval, and loving concern from parents is likely to conclude that he or she is a valued person and thereby develops a positive self-concept and high self-esteem. Such messages to the child may be very direct, as when a parent says, "You're a great kid and I love you very much," or they may be transmitted in more subtle ways, such as approving smiles and expressions of attention and interest in the child. On the other hand, children who receive a lot of disapproval, rejection, and hostility from those who matter are likely to infer that others see them as unlovable, unworthy, and inferior. It is not surprising that such children tend to develop negative self-concepts and low self-esteem.

There is a second important type of information that enters into the developing conception of self. At a relatively early age, children begin to compare themselves with other children. This is quite natural, for in any new or novel situation we have little basis for judging ourselves or our performance except in comparison with others. Social comparison and competition begin around the age of four or five. There is an increase in the need to compare and compete throughout the elementary school years, with the peak occurring around grades four, five, and six.

Through self-comparison and competition with other children, youngsters learn where they stand relative to others like them. It is easy to see how such information would feed into the developing self-concept of the child and how important it is for parents to help the child understand and evaluate such information.

It is important to realize that the way any experience affects a child's self-concept depends on several factors. The child's already existing self-concept is one of the most important. Psychologists who study personality place such emphasis on self-concept because it affects how we process new information. We tend to filter information and to behave in accordance with our self-concept. We accept evidence that supports our notion of ourselves, be it positive or negative, and reject or devalue evidence that is inconsistent with our self-concept. Thus, a failure may have little impact on a child with a positive view of himself or herself, while the same failure may serve to demonstrate once again to the low-self-esteem youngster how inadequate he or she really is. Low-self-esteem children have little confidence in their abilities. They are insecure in their relationships with others, are highly sensitive to criticism, and are easily hurt. Some try to cover up their feelings of inadequacy with an aggressive or attention-demanding front that alienates others, whereas others withdraw into a protective shell. Either response tends to result in low popularity, and this only serves to confirm a poor self-image. The low-self-esteem youngster is thus primed for entry into a failure cycle.

Another factor determining the impact of success or failure on a child's developing self-concept is the importance of the activity. Success in an area that is important to a child, be it academic, social, or athletic, has a stronger positive impact than does success in an activity that does not matter. Likewise, failure in an important area has a stronger negative impact.

Considering the factors we have discussed so far helps us to understand why sport experiences can have an important effect on a child's self-concept. Children typically enter the world of sports at a time in their development when they are seeking information about their abilities. The kinds of motor abilities required in sports are particularly valued by them at this stage. When children enter sports, the stage is thus set for an ability test whose outcome is potentially very important.

Children enter sports for a variety of reasons. Most of their friends and acquaintances are playing, so it's the "in" thing to do as well as a good way to make new friends or participate in a new activity with old friends. Many parents are also clearly interested in sports and therefore encourage or, at times, pressure their children to participate. Finally, sports are an enjoyable, challenging activity in their own right. Whether some or all of these factors bring a child into a program, it is clear that the activity is important to someone in the child's life, including, usually, the child.

There are also good reasons to try to succeed and to be a good athlete. Success brings feelings of mastery, competence and self-pride, admiration and status from peers, and approval from important adults, such as parents and coaches. Inferior athletes often experience feelings of shame and inferiority, lowered respect and status among their peers, and the reactions of disappointed parents.

At the very first practice or tryout, children begin to see how they compare with their peers in this prized activity. In a very short time children can tell how proficient they are relative to their teammates and opponents.

In addition to comparing themselves with others, children also have many opportunities to observe how others are judging them. The reactions of coaches, parents, teammates, opponents, and spectators to their play are visible on many occasions. Some of these evaluations are very direct, as when others offer praise or criticism. Other reactions, although unintentionally shown, are easily picked up by a child. For example, when Bobby comes to the plate with the bases loaded, his teammates, coach, and the spectators cheer and shout encouragement. When Chad comes up under the same circumstances, there is silence or maybe even a few groans. Or "encouragement" may take such forms as "C'mon, Chad, try to hit the ball!" or "Don't strike out!"

As youth sport programs become more highly organized, formal procedures, such as grading players during tryouts, "drafting" players, and even buying them with play money, provide direct indications of ability. One child we know was devastated when his coach paid only $25,000 in play money for him while his neighborhood buddy went for $40,000! Even more painful is being cut, a most humiliating message that one doesn't measure up. Research done in Canada by sport scientist Terry Orlick showed that nearly three out of every four nonparticipants didn't go out for hockey teams because they feared not being good enough to make a team — an indication of how much children dread the message that they're not good enough.

Even children who make the team continue to receive many messages about their performance. This feedback comes from people whose opinions carry a great deal of weight because they are so important to the child. Many parents are very concerned about their children's athletic development and often have a good deal to say about performance. It is the job of another significant adult, the coach, to evaluate performance. Youngsters receive much feedback from this "expert" about their strengths, weaknesses, areas needing improvement, and progress. The coach also makes very obvious ability judgments in selecting players for particular positions, in choosing who starts and who substitutes, and in deciding the game conditions in which substitutions occur. Being allowed to play only when one's team is way ahead or hopelessly behind communications a pretty clear message.

To summarize, then, the athletic arena provides many opportunities for children to form judgments of their abilities. They get information by comparing themselves with others as well as by observing the reactions of others to them. All this occurs during the age period when children are beginning to form a stable conception of who they are and how they feel about themselves. If you add to this the fact that motor abilities are of central importance and highly valued at this age and that the people evaluating the child — coaches, peers, and parents — are of great importance in the child's life, is it any wonder why the experiences children have in sports can have a rather profound effect on them? This is particularly the case with children who have not established feelings of self-worth in other areas of their lives or with those whose parents value athletic abilities above all others. Finally it is important to realize that children at this age are not yet capable of distinguishing between judgments of their abilities and judgments of their personal worth. Thus, ability judgments are not necessarily seen as evaluations of only a single physical trait but may well be taken as an indication of total worth.

It is important that adults be sensitive to the impact that sport experiences can have on the child's developing conception of self. The processes we have described — self-comparison and feedback from others — are going to occur in any situation in which children interact, but their effects can be softened and viewed more realistically if understanding adults help children place sport experiences in proper perspective. There are several things adults can do.

First and foremost is to emphasize fun, participation, and skill improvement rather than winning and losing. Most children want to play a sport because they enjoy the activity for its own sake. When adults turn that enjoyable activity into a pressurized, competitive nightmare, the child's intrinsic desire to play can recede into the background. Fun is no longer just playing; it's now defined as winning. Introducing material rewards, such as trophies, into the picture can cause children to lose sight of the fun of merely playing.

Second, adults should emphasize striving to improve skills rather than comparing oneself with others. Physical development and skill development occur at different rates in youngsters, and it is important to make this clear to children. It is particularly important that children whose skill development is lagging not view this as a permanent condition. Helping a youngster derive pleasure from his or her improvement over time and praising the self-improvement efforts of the child create many rewarding experiences in sport, even for the athlete who never will be a star.

Just as it is important that the unskilled child athlete not develop low self-worth because of his or her own sport abilities, it is important that the highly skilled athlete not acquire an inflated self-image. Again, helping children to understand that despite the importance of sport to them, it is only one area of their lives will foster a more balanced perspective and a wider range of interests.

Finally, it is important that parents examine the conditions of worth that they hold for their children. If your young athlete must excel to get love and approval from you, if you are sending out subtle (or not so subtle) signals of disapproval when your child fails or embarrasses you, then you need to take a hard look at your own priorities. If, on the other hand, you are able to communicate love and acceptance to your child whether he or she is a star or a bench warmer, then a basis for positive self-concept development exists regardless of your child's eventual success in sports.

Competitive experiences are an important part of life. In themselves, sports are neither good nor bad. The value of competition for the child depends on how the competition is conducted, how the situation is interpreted, and how the outcome of competition is understood. Properly managed, youth sports can be an important training ground for competing successfully in other areas of life and for the development of a positive self-concept.

Sport Motivation and Competitiveness

The concept of motivation is the central one in our attempt to understand the whys of behavior. It helps us to understand differences among people in the goals they pursue and in the vigor and persistence with which they pursue them. In sport as in other areas of life, the importance of motivation is well recognized. Motivation is crucial to understanding both sport involvement and performance. As a parent, understanding your child's needs and motives can help you provide a more positive athletic experience for him or her.

There are many reasons why children are drawn to sport. Some of the reasons are inherent in the activities themselves. Children, like adults, find it enjoyable to hit a baseball, dribble and shoot a basketball, run and catch a football, kick a soccer ball, or stroke a tennis ball. Using one's body just for the sake of doing so is in itself a joyful activity and provides what psychologists term *intrinsic* motives for participating in sports.

Sport involvement can also be a means of satisfying other important needs. We have already talked about the need to compare ourselves with others in the process of defining our abilities and establishing our self-concept. There are two other psychological needs that sport fulfills: the need for competence and achievement, and the need for recognition and approval.

Achievement-Related Motives

Sport provides many opportunities to demonstrate competence and mastery. It is an area in which competence is highly valued by adults and children alike. We should therefore expect that motives having to do with success and failure would be among the most important determinants of sport participation and performance.

The most universal principle of motivation is that people, like animals, strive for positive or pleasurable things and avoid experiences that are painful or threatening. Motivation theorists thus distinguish between *approach* motives and *avoidance* motives. In achievement there are two separate but related motives: the need to achieve, and fear of failure. Research has shown quite clearly that these are separate sources of motivation and that people differ widely in the strength of these two motivational states. Some people are low in both motives, others are high in one and low in the other, and still others are high in both.

The need to achieve is an approach motive. It is a positive desire to attain success and to compete successfully with standards of excellence. Differences in achievement motivation begin to emerge in children in the early school years. Children who are high in achievement motivation seek out challenging situations and are concerned with how well they perform, in terms of both their own standards and the performance of others. They also tend to show a lot of persistence in their attempts to achieve. Failure tends to spur them on to greater effort rather than discourage them. They tend to prefer situations that put their abilities to the test. Many studies have shown that when their achievement motivation is aroused, these children perform at a higher level than those low in achievement motivation. Interestingly, they do not perform better if they do not view the situation as an opportunity to achieve.

The other side of the achievement coin is, of course, failure. Just as some children show a positive desire for success, others exhibit a negative fear of failure. People who have great fear of failure work hard not so much because they yearn for "the thrill of victory" as because they dread "the agony of defeat." For them, achievement situations are not challenges, but threats. The child highly motivated to achieve gets "pumped" and "psyched up" when faced with a challenge, but the child highly motivated by the fear of failure is more likely to get "psyched out." Tension, fear, and anxiety result. And although the motivation to achieve tends to improve performance, the fear of failure tends to disrupt it.

Competitiveness

One of the most highly prized athletic traits is competitiveness. Applying what we now know about achievement-related motives helps us to understand what goes into being a good competitor. From youth leagues to professional leagues, outstanding competitors are almost always people who are high in achievement motivation and low in fear of failure. Challenging athletic situations arouse their strong desire to achieve, and unhindered by performance-disrupting fears of failure, they tend to peak under

Relationships Between Achievement Motivation, Fear of Failure, and Competitiveness

		Achievement Motivation	
		Low	*High*
Fear of Failure	*Low*	Achievement concerns are largely irrelevant. Appears "laid back" and is probably in sport for reasons unrelated to achievement.	Is a good competitor; peaks under pressure because fear of failure does not disrupt performance. Enjoys and seeks out the challenges of competition and is persistently motivated to win.
	High	Competition is threatening. Experiences anxiety under pressure, which lowers performance. Does not enjoy competition and may avoid such situations by dropping out.	Has conflict in competitive situations. Wants to win but also fears failure, so performance may suffer. Does not enjoy the threatening part of competition.

pressure. They enjoy and seek out the challenge of athletic competition.

Quite the opposite occurs in the child who is primarily motivated by fear of failure. Competitive situations provide little to gain but much to lose for such children. If they can avoid competition, they will do so. If other factors force them to compete, they derive little enjoyment from it and their performance tends to deteriorate under pressure. Some children who apparently enjoy sports but who have a great fear of failure tend to like practices and "goofing off" more than they do games.

Besides children with such high-low levels of achievement motivation and fear of failure, there are also children who have high levels of both and those who have low levels of both. The child who has high levels of both motives is in a state of conflict between approach and avoidance motives. This child wants to achieve but also fears failure. If the child enjoys the sport itself, he or she tends to remain in it but experiences stress and anxiety under pressure. The key to helping such a child to become a good competitor is to reduce his or her fear of failure so that the positive effects of the motivation to achieve are not interfered with.

For the child who has low levels of both achievement motivation and fear of failure, achievement concerns have little importance. When such children do elect to participate in sports, it is often because they simply enjoy the activity or because of the social benefits of participation. As a result, they exhibit a rather nonchalant attitude about the sport. This can prove perplexing and irritating to parents and coaches who are more concerned about winning and achievement.

Because the motivation to achieve and the fear of failure so strongly affect enjoyment of and performance in achievement situations, researchers have been very interested in understanding how these motives develop. They have found that children who have high levels of achievement motivation but little fear of failure tend to have a history of encouragement and reward for success and independence. Parents of such children tend to emphasize the positive aspects of achievement and to praise their children for their efforts to achieve. Importantly, when their children try hard but nevertheless fail, these parents do not punish or criticize them. Instead, they encourage them to continue their attempts and praise them for their persistence. Because of the emphasis that the parents place on striving to meet standards of excellence, this value is adopted by the children and serves to guide their behavior.

The background of the fear-of-failure child is quite different. These children tend to want to avoid new experiences or activities because of the punishment or rejection associated with previous failures. Their parents tend to focus only on the success or failure experienced by the child, not on the effort the child puts out. They express displeasure with the child when failure occurs but take success for granted and expect it. In other instances unrealistically high goals are set for the child, and the parents express displeasure when the child does not succeed. It is quite easy to see how such a background would result in a child who has learned to dread failure. Ironically, once the fear develops, its disruptive effects are likely to decrease still further the chances of success. What often occurs is a vicious cycle in which failure results in increased anxiety, which in turn helps to ensure future failure.

Sport can be a training ground for the development of positive motivation toward achievement. Parents and coaches can have an important influence on developing attitudes concerning success and failure. Research on the development of the need for achievement and fear of failure offers some pretty clear guidelines for how you can help your child develop a healthy achievement orientation. The key principles seem to be encouraging the child to give maximum effort and rewarding him or her for that effort. Make sure the achievement standards you set are reasonable and within your child's capabilities. When success occurs, enjoy the success with your child and express appreciation for the effort that went into it. *Never* be punitive or rejecting if the child tries but does not succeed. Show your child that you understand how disappointed he or she is, and encourage the child to continue trying. Communicate love and acceptance regardless of success or failure. If you want to avoid developing fear of failure, don't give your child a reason to dread failure.

Needs for Approval and Recognition

As social beings we humans are deeply concerned about the reactions of others to us. We seem to have an inborn need to be recognized, valued, and cared about by others. From a very early age, children seem to crave attention and to do whatever is necessary to gain it. Many children with behavior problems develop those problems because obnoxious behavior is the only way the children have of guaranteeing the attention of parents and others. Such children prefer the attention that goes along with being punished to simply being ignored.

As children develop they learn to satisfy their needs for recognition and approval in a variety of ways. For one thing, they find out what is praiseworthy to people who matter to them, such as parents, teachers, and peers. It doesn't take most children very long to realize that sports provide many opportunities for recognition and approval. They see how sports heroes are idolized in our culture, and they often develop their own sports heroes at a relatively early age. Further, many parents communicate very positive attitudes about sports and exhibit a great deal of interest in such activities, either as participants or as spectators. Finally, as we noted earlier, physical skills are among the most highly prized attributes of school-aged children.

Approval and recognition provide powerful motivation for athletes at all levels. Almost all of the positive attributes that can be developed through sports participation — achievement motivation, sportsmanship, teamwork, unselfishness — are ultimately strengthened through the approval of significant people, such as coaches, parents, and teammates. Thus, it is almost impossible to overestimate the importance of approval and recognition to the developing athlete.

As was the case with achievement, there are both approach and avoidance motives connected with approval. On the approach side, there is the positive desire to obtain approval and recognition from other people. This is similar to the positive achievement motive that we discussed earlier. The child wants approval and may be frustrated if approval is not received, but the child is not necessarily afraid of disapproval.

On the other hand, the social behavior of many people is motivated by a strong desire to avoid disapproval at all costs, a motivational state similar to fear of failure. Such people are very concerned about the evaluation of others, and they are fearful of being evaluated unfavorably. Often they automatically assume that all assessments will be negative. As a result, they may experience considerable tension and distress in social situations, and they may be highly motivated to avoid them. Where fear of disapproval is not excessive, these people enter social situations but strive to please others at all costs. They are highly conforming and hesitate to take a position that others might disapprove of. They define their own self-worth in terms of the feedback they get from other people.

For the child athlete the most important external sources of approval are coaches, parents, and peers. Of equally great importance, however, is the child's own approval or disapproval of himself or herself. Once children begin to set standards for their own behavior, they approve or disapprove of themselves depending on whether or not they meet these standards. Thus, a young boy may feel badly about himself if he does something that he knows is wrong even if his friends approve. The development of internal standards of behavior and of conditions for self-approval and self-disapproval is a sign of developing maturity in a child.

Motivational patterns differ from child to child, of course, but in a recent research project we tried to determine the relative strength of approval motives in child athletes. We devised a psychological test to measure the approval-related reasons that children strive to do well in sports, and we administered the test to a large number of boys and girls of various ages.

The following table shows the results of this study.

Reasons for Trying to Perform Well in Sports

Reason for Trying to Play Well	Order of Importance	
	9–11 Years Old	*12–14 Years Old*
1. Feeling good about how you played.	1	1
2. Making sure you won't blame yourself for losing.	2	2
3. Being praised by your parents for playing well.	6	4
4. Making sure your parents won't be displeased with your play.	3	8
5. Making your coach proud of you.	4	3
6. Making sure your coach won't be displeased with you.	5	6
7. Making the other kids like you more.	8	7
8. Making sure the other kids don't get upset with you.	7	5

It is noteworthy that for children in both age groups, their own self-approval and disapproval were more important to them than the reactions of peers, coaches, or parents. Where parents were concerned, the younger children were more strongly oriented toward avoiding parental disapproval than toward gaining their approval, whereas the older youngsters were relatively more concerned with getting approval than with avoiding disapproval.

The motives that bring children into sport and that affect their development and performance once they are involved are of great importance in understanding the child athlete. In subsequent chapters we will return frequently to these motivational factors.

Extrinsic Motivation: Can We Destroy Love of the Game?

The story is told of an elderly woman who lived in an apartment building next to a vacant lot. One afternoon just as she was settling down for her daily nap, an exuberant group of boys and girls appeared in the vacant lot and began a noisy pickup softball game. The din was deafening and the children obviously enjoyed the game far more than the old woman did. Her only solace was the hope that they would not come back. But, alas, the children joyfully returned the next two days as well.

On the third day, as the children were leaving, the woman walked down to the vacant lot and called them together. She told them that she liked to watch and listen to them play and asked them to come back and play noisily in the vacant lot the next day. If they did, she said, she would give each of them a quarter. The children raced back the following day and had a noisy game, looking occasionally up at the old woman smiling approvingly from her window. She paid each of them a quarter and asked them to return the next day. Again the next day she paid them after their game. This time, however, she gave each child only twenty cents, explaining that she was running out of money. On the following day, they got only fifteen cents each. Furthermore, she told them, she would have to reduce their payment to five cents the next day. The children became angry and told the woman they would not be back. It was not worth the effort, they said, to play a game for her for only five cents a day.

The old woman might very well have been a retired psychologist, for she had cleverly used external rewards, in this case money, to decrease the desire of children to play ball. We can assume that the children originally came to the vacant lot because of their intrinsic motivation to play softball "for the fun of it." When money was introduced into the picture as an additional reward for playing, the children began to see themselves as playing primarily to get this extrinsic reward. Once this shift in their perception of their own motives occurred, the withdrawal of the money reduced their desire to play.

Although this story is probably fictional, the principle that extrinsic rewards can undermine intrinsic motivation is not. Psychological experiments have continually shown that this can occur in children and adults alike. In youth sports there is the risk that children's intrinsic interest in the sport can be decreased if they begin to see their participation as a means to some extrinsic goals, such as trophies, trips, or state championships.

If carried to an extreme, external rewards can replace intrinsic motivation as the reason for participating in sports. When the young athletes begin to see these extrinsic rewards as the reason for their participation, the removal of these rewards may result in a loss of interest in participation.

An unhappy example of exactly this effect is the case of the teenage wrestler whose father called one of us recently. The father was very concerned because his young athlete refused to enter meets unless the winners' trophies were large enough to justify the effort.

We are not suggesting that trophies and other extrinsic rewards be eliminated from sports. They certainly have their rightful place as a means of recognizing outstanding effort and achievement. It is important, however, that adults and children maintain a proper perspective so that trophies do not become the be-all and end-all of participation. It is sad indeed when children lose the capacity to enjoy playing the game for its own sake.

Sports and Character-Building

Raising our children is in large part a moral enterprise. We do our best to teach our children the difference between right and wrong. We communicate our own values to them and hope they will adopt similar values. We want them to develop positive character traits that will make them happy and contributing members of society. Our goals in this regard are shared by religious institutions, schools, youth organizations, and athletic programs. The motto of Little League Baseball—"Character, Courage, Loyalty"—exemplifies the commitment that many youth sport programs have made to develop sportsmanship and good citizenship. Adult leadership responsibilities in such programs go beyond teaching sport skills to include stressing the value of hard work, sportsmanship, and good citizenship. As one Little League Baseball official told us, "Little League Baseball has nothing to do with baseball."

Not everyone agrees that youth sport programs succeed in these goals. Critics point out that in some instances impressionable youngsters learn to swear, cheat, fight, intimidate, and hurt others. Sports provide opportunities to learn immoral values and behaviors as well as moral ones. Depending on the types of leadership provided by coaches and parents, the experiences can result in sinners as well as saints. In the final analysis it is not the sport itself that automatically determines the worth of the activity for the child, but rather the nature of the experiences within the program.

Sport is an especially promising setting for learning the positive traits we lump under the term *character,* because it confronts children with many challenges that await them in later life. Cooperation, competition, perseverance in the face of difficulties, concern for others, self-sacrifice, and moral behavior (sportsmanship) can all be called for on any given day. Through the influence they have as important adults in children's lives, coaches and parents can teach children to respond to these challenges in desirable ways. Important lessons of life can be learned on the athletic field and in the gymnasium.

The Coach As Moral Philosopher

The youth sport coach is charged with teaching children not only the skills of the sport but also the value of hard work, sportsmanship, and good citizenship. To study the communication of moral values, University of Minnesota sociologist Gary Fine and his colleagues observed youth baseball coaches over a three-year period. Among the themes that the coaches stressed were effort, sportsmanship, and teamwork. Here are some examples:

> Your goal for the year is to be a winner. That doesn't mean winning every game. Sometimes you will be up against teams that are better than you. It does mean to give everything you've got. If you give everything that you've got, you're a winner in my book. The only one who cares is the Man that made you and He made both teams, both winners and losers. Give everything you've got.

Coach after his team (with a 6–3 record) loses 5–1:

> You guys are sleeping out there. If you have no pride in yourself, I don't want you . . . In other games, even in games in which you guys won, there was a lack of hustle . . . I won't quit on you, don't quit on me.
>
> Guys, you got a big lead—I don't want any monkeying around out there, I want no talking to them. I want you to be good sports.

Coach after come-from-behind victory:

> Isn't that nice to come back and win it? It was a team effort. Everybody played well.

Suppose that we view sports as a setting where adults can influence children to think, believe, feel, and behave in certain ways. There are basically three ways in which children can respond to attempts at social influence: compliance, identification, or internalization. Different kinds of motivation underlie each type of response, and responses differ in their permanence.

Compliance refers to responses that are made solely to obtain a reward or to avoid punishment. Thus, a coach who is trying to teach players sportsmanship may threaten them with punishment for heckling opponents. If the punishment is severe enough, players may behave well in this regard. But as we might expect, their compliance will not necessarily endure. In the coach's absence, they may quickly revert to unsportsmanlike heckling. They will not have grasped and accepted the principle underlying the coach's demands.

A stronger and more permanent response to social influence occurs in *identification*. Identification results from a child's desire to be like another person or to be identified with a particular group. Thus, if the children admire and want to be like the coach, and if the coach consistently emphasizes and practices sportsmanship, then the children may behave in a similar manner. It is important to realize, however, that children's sportsmanship does not necessarily reflect their own values. If for some reason the children stop identifying with the coach, the adopted behaviors may disappear.

Internalization is the most permanent and deeply rooted response to social influence. When children internalize values and behavior, they take them on as their own because they believe they are correct or proper. Internalized values and behavior do not depend upon subsequent rewards and punishments, nor do they require that the child continue to identify with the person who influenced him or her. They are maintained because the child believes that they are right.

Obviously, internalization is the hoped-for result of our attempts to teach children desirable attitudes and behaviors. In bringing these behaviors about, it is important that we explain to children the principles or reasons behind desired actions. For example, rather than simply threatening to punish players for heckling opponents, a coach might help his players understand the golden rule "Do unto others as you would have them do unto you" by asking them to consider what it would be like to be the victims of heckling — and thus encourage his players to develop empathy for their opponents. This ability to place oneself in the role of another person is essential to the development of morality. Understanding and applying this golden rule can lead children to internalize the concept of sportsmanship and consideration for others.

Youngsters learn moral behavior not only through verbal explanations, rewards, and punishments but also by observing how other people behave. They imitate their parents and peers, and they model themselves after their heroes. Because coaches are often highly admired and very important in the child's life, they are especially likely to serve as models. Without realizing it, coaches can behave in ways that teach either morality or immorality. For example, by trying to get the edge by stretching the rules, coaches can easily give children the impression that cheating is not really wrong unless it is detected, and then only to the extent that it hurts the chances of winning. When coaches bend the rules in order to obtain a victory, children may conclude that the end justifies the means. Likewise, coaches who display hostility toward officials and contempt for the other team communicate the notion that such behaviors are appropriate and desirable. Even when coaches and parents preach correct values, it is essential that they themselves behave in accordance with them. Psychological experiments with children have repeatedly shown that when adults' actions are inconsistent with their words, it is the actions, not the words, that influence children's behavior. Actions do indeed speak louder than words.

Critics of youth sports sometimes attack the competitive aspect of sports as inconsistent with the development of morality and concern for others. Some, however, dispute this position, arguing that moral development is actually furthered when moral decisions come into conflict with winning. In other words, noteworthy acts of sportsmanship often involve situations in which conduct governed by a moral principle (for example, that one should not cheat) is chosen instead of victory. When a youngster makes a decision to do the right thing rather than unfairly pursue an opportunity to succeed, we have a true demonstration of moral growth. Coaches and parents are in a position to further such growth.

What, then, is the verdict on sports as a means of building character? At this point we are unable to give a definite answer, for sport is simply one aspect of the complexity of children's lives. Scientific evidence is inconclusive, although positive differences in academic achievement and personality traits are sometimes found when groups of child athletes are compared with nonathletes. A lower incidence of juvenile delinquency has consistently been found in child athletes. The difficulty has been in proving that these differences are caused by sports participation. Perhaps brighter and better-adjusted children are more likely to be attracted to sports, and that's why participation is related to these attributes. There is no denying, however, that sports are capable of furthering the character development of children if adults are able to structure sports experiences for their benefit. The sport experience is full of valuable lessons for children and can be an important training ground for moral and social development.

3

Physical Development

Trying Out Some New Equipment

The body of the athlete determines his or her athletic potential and has much to do with how much enjoyment and satisfaction can come from training and competition. The 126-pound high school boy trying to fill out a football uniform with little more than the skin and bones of a slowly maturing adolescent cannot contribute a star performance to the team, nor is he going to remember that one of the highs of his young life was playing football. He would probably be happy to trade in his current body model for something closer to six feet in height, 180 pounds in weight, and equipped with a well-developed set of muscles.

Body structure and function are important in determining how satisfying and enjoyable a sport experience can be. For example, in sports such as football, wrestling, and ice hockey, an athlete's body characteristics have a lot to do with how safe the sport is.

What are the features of body structure that affect sports participation? Height is an obviously important characteristic. There is always one five-foot, eight-inch guard in a high school basketball tournament, but the six-foot, six-inch player is ten inches closer to the basket and has a better chance of scoring more points. Weight is another aspect of body size that is a determinant of potential success. The two-hundred-pound tackle has a distinct playing advantage over an opponent who weighs only two thirds as much.

Body build, or physique, must also be considered. The three major body types (somatotypes) are *endomorphs,* characterized by a soft roundness throughout the body, with a tendency toward fatness; *mesomorphs,* muscular individuals with large, prominent bones; and *ectomorphs,* who have thin body segments and poor muscle development. Successful athletes in a particular sport tend to have similar body builds, and their physiques are compatible with the requirements of the activity. Being a mesomorph or an ectomorph will have a lot to do with whether an individual must be satisfied with recreation jogging or will enjoy working his or her long, thin legs in competitive distance races. But having a certain body type does not guarantee success or failure. The outcome is not absolute. With this in mind you can help your child select sports that are compatible with his or her body build. This will give your child a better chance to achieve higher levels of performance.

In addition to body size and build, athletic performance is influenced by body composition—the relative amounts of bone, muscle, and fat that make up body mass. The role of muscle in moving the body and generating force is of prime importance. Quite simply, the more strength and power that an athlete has, the greater his or her advantage will be. On the other hand, fatty tissue represents excess baggage and is a performance-inhibitor. Fatness reduces speed, limits endurance and, in some sports, increases the risk of injury. In almost all sports, with the exception of sumo wrestling perhaps, elite athletes strive to be trim and muscular, with healthy minimal levels of body fat.

The physical characteristics that determine sport performance are constantly changing during the growing years of childhood and adolescence. Knowing something about normal growth will tell us much about what kind of athletic activity might be appropriate for different ages. In other words, knowledge of the nature and extent of growth will help answer crucial questions about what sport for what child at what age. With such information, it is possible to project realistic expectations of sport performance on our children and to direct them into training programs that their changing bodies will respond to. As boys and girls move through the exciting stages of growing up in sport, some appreciation of the ever-changing body can make the experience the satisfying one it should be.

Factors That Influence Body Characteristics

With the exception of identical twins, no two human bodies are exactly the same. Body size, shape, and composition, as well as the body's million physiological characteristics, are unique to each individual. These physical attributes are influenced by age and sex, along with a host of internal and external (environmental) factors. For example, the endocrine glands secrete hormones directly into the bloodstream. Hormones are basically regulators of body functions, and they play an important role in physical growth and sexual maturation. With respect to environmental forces, body structure and function depend on how adequate nutrition has been, how free from disease the body has been, and how physically active one has been.

Most importantly, body characteristics are determined by genetic factors. Certainly we know that parent height is a prime determinant of offspring height. Hereditary influences on body structure and its many functions are so important in determining the potential for athletic performance that it is often said that great athletes are born, not made. The significance of one's genetic endowment cannot be denied.

Aside from the size, shape, and makeup of the body, there are several ways in which body functions respond to exercise and training that are important contributors to athletic performance. As with the body's structure, these abilities to respond to training are in large part determined by genetic characteristics. They include the potential for developing outstanding muscle strength as well as the capabilities of producing muscle energy efficiently and of increasing the body's metabolism to a very high level to meet the demands of vigorous exercise. There are nervous-system functions responsible for effective information-processing in training muscle responses. Quick reaction and speed of movement are important to the athlete, as are the potentials for speed and quickness. These traits are all inheritable. If someone wishes to develop the body of an elite athlete and the potential to respond ideally to a proper training program for a particular sport, the individual should begin by selecting his or her parents with great care.

We've emphasized that hereditary factors are critical in determining which children can look forward to being outstanding, and perhaps even elite, athletes. However, the effects of genetics are never absolute, because genes do not operate in isolation. We cannot discount the influence of the environments in which we live, natural, manmade, and social. Regular exercise, active muscle work, is among the many environmental factors essential during childhood and adolescence to achieve full potential for growth. Moderate physical stress from the activities found in most sport programs is generally a positive force on bone growth. Yet it is doubtful whether training programs for young athletes have any influence on their height. Dramatic exercise effects do, however, occur in muscle and adipose (fat) tissue. Following the onset of adolescence in the male, the increase in size of muscle cells, and consequently the increase in muscle mass, is directly related to the intensity and duration of the training program. And, of course, the loss of fatty tissue from exercise is a desirable effect of sport involvement.

On the side of caution, relatively little is known about the limits beyond which strenuous physical activity can be harmful to a young athlete's growth. Unfortunately, there is no exact guide for determining how much activity is appropriate. The issue includes consideration of the maturation level of the child and the frequency and duration of the activity. The most reasonable approach is to rely on the child's own tolerance; the young athlete will generally know when his or her limit has been reached. Later in this chapter, we will discuss the maturity level at which a young boy or girl can expect to respond to endurance and strength training.

A related and equally important issue concerns the exercise tolerance of healthy children. Do endurance sports place *excessive* demands on the hearts of young athletes? No. This is a popular myth. There is considerable evidence that the growing child's heart responds favorably to physical exertion. In fact, a child's exercise tolerance is greater than believed in the past. The key to safely handling the demands of heavy exercise resides in the health of the child. This points to the necessity of careful medical screening, which includes probing for a family history of cardiac problems and any early cardiovascular difficulties. Also, in protecting the wellness of child athletes, parents cannot ignore the importance of appropriate endurance-training procedures.

Today's Body Types

Children are growing to a larger size and maturing more rapidly than ever before. The following figure shows how fifteen-year-old boys have attained progressively greater height and weight during recent decades. American boys and girls from essentially all economic groups have experienced a similar increase in their rate of growth and size during the past two generations. It now appears that for the most privileged in our society, the full genetic potential for size and rate of growth has been achieved; future generations are not expected to grow faster or be larger. Better nutrition, freedom from most diseases, and a generally healthier environment are prompting children to greater growth performances than experienced by their ancestors.

As can be seen in the figure, as children grew larger, there was an associated increase in physical performance. The bigger they became, the farther they were able to jump because of greater muscle strength. Today's boys and girls can jump farther and are stronger than their fathers and mothers were at the same age. It is

Growth and Performance Increases in Young Boys between 1923 and 1969–70. For Height, 2.54 cm = 1 inch; for Weight, 1 kg = 2.20 pounds.

Improvements in Performances for Various Olympic Events				
Event	Males		Females	
	Year Introduced	%	Year Introduced	%
100m	1896	16.2	1928	9.2
200m	1900	8.9	1948	8.3
400m	1896	18.3		
800m	1896	21.8	1928	16.0
1500m	1896	19.8		
High Jump	1896	24.3	1928	21.4
Long Jump	1896	31.5	1948	18.1
Triple Jump	1896	26.1		
Shotput	1896	87.6	1948	53.9
Discus	1896	131.6	1928	74.2
Javelin	1908	72.5	1932	51.0

Percentages are calculated from the winning times and distances for each event reported in de Groote (1975) and Comité Organisateur des Jeux de la XXIe Olympiade (1976a).

interesting to look at the improvement in records set in the Olympic Games since they were inaugurated just prior to the turn of the century. The table above shows the improvement in performance in various track-and-field events. Improved coaching, equipment, and facilities have all contributed to these performance changes, but because of greater growth rates and larger sizes, bigger and stronger athletes have been competing. As expected with bigger, stronger athletes, the greatest improvement in record performances has occurred in those events most directly dependent on strength, such as the shot put and discus.

Those responsible for sports programs for children and youth must recognize that athletes in our sports programs are a different population from those of a generation or two ago. Athletes today are bigger and stronger at younger ages. Particularly at the junior and senior high school levels, the "new model" athletes will not only perform better, they will demand a higher degree of sophistication and concern in dealing with their protective equipment, training facilities, coaching, refereeing, and even rule changes. Today's young athletes have an increased potential for causing and sustaining injuries, and their programs must command a higher level of support and attention to safety than was needed in the past.

Patterns of Physical Growth

There is an abundance of information concerning the growth of American children. Growth can be looked at merely as heights or weights for given ages, as seen in the following figure. This type of curve (a distance curve) indicates a child's growth status, or the size attained at a particular age. It is interesting to look at the increases in height and weight that occur during a given period of time.

The velocity curve shown in the next figure illustrates the rate of growth, that is, centimeters or kilograms gained per year. We can see that the most rapid period of growth occurs immediately after birth, and then the growth rate slows to a modest, steady process during childhood. This is followed by an adolescent growth spurt and then by deceleration until growth finally stops. There is little difference in the relative rates of growth of boys and girls during childhood. However, as shown in the first figure, during childhood boys are slightly taller and heavier than girls of the same age. This difference is a relatively minor one and of no real practical significance for sport performance.

When girls experience the rapid growth spurt that occurs between the ages of ten and a half and thirteen, they become taller than boys. During pubescence tall girls will be taller than tall boys, and all girls will be taller than the shortest 3 to 5 percent of boys. This is a temporary situation that changes when boys begin to experience their adolescent growth spurt in height some two years after girls have experienced their peak velocity in gaining height.

Prior to adolescence, sex differences in body composition are minor. However, boys do have slightly more bone and muscle tissue and less fat than girls. Following the period of maximum gain in height that occurs in early adolescence (about age twelve to thirteen for girls and fourteen to fifteen for boys), there is a period of maximum gain in weight. In girls this is due primarily to a large increase in body fat, with a relatively small increase in muscle tissue. In boys the rapid gain in body weight that follows a rapid gain in height is due to a decrease in body fatness and a striking increase in muscle mass. Consequently, postadolescent girls have only about two thirds as much muscle as males, and young adult females have almost twice the amount of body fat.

Because boys on the average begin their rapid gain in height at the age of twelve and a half, they have about two more years of

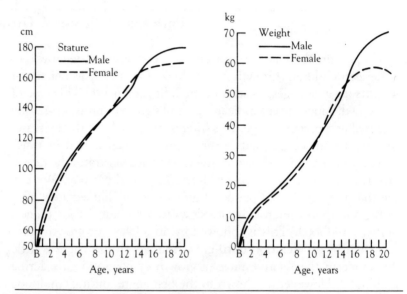

Typical Growth in Height and Weight for Boys and Girls. For Height, 2.54 cm = 1 inch; for Weight, 1 kg = 2.20 pounds.

Velocity Curves Showing Rates of Increase in Height and Weight

preadolescent growth than girls have. During this two-year period they continue to grow, and at age fourteen or fifteen they are about four inches taller than girls were when they began their rapid growth. In the immediate preadolescent period, boys' legs grow much faster than their trunks. Thus, the longer period of preadolescent growth for males is responsible for the fact that legs of adult males are longer than those of females. Prior to puberty other body measures, such as arm length and shoulder and hip width, are not significantly different.

The age at which the adolescent growth spurt begins varies considerably from one child to another. The variation is so great in a sample of normal males, for example, that some boys may have their most rapid growth as early as their twelfth birthday whereas others will not have this growth experience until they are nearly sixteen. These slower-maturing boys will not have their muscle growth and rapid gain in body weight until more than fourteen months later, at seventeen or eighteen years of age. A very normal but slowly maturing young male will have completed high school before he is physically suited to compete in many sports requiring large size, strength, and a mature skeleton.

The differences in age at which adolescent growth and physical development occur are most evident during junior high school or middle school, or at twelve to fifteen years of age. Normal boys can vary as much as fifteen inches in height, a hundred pounds in weight, and five years in maturation status, that is, biologic age. (Biologic age is commonly determined by an X-ray examination of skeletal maturation.) As long as most school-based sports programs and the majority of community-based sports match competitors on the basis of calendar age, large numbers of boys who do not experience their growth and maturation close to the average risk some very significant problems. This is true for both the slow later maturer and the advanced early maturer. We will address these specific concerns later in this chapter.

Changes in Physical Abilities During Childhood and Adolescence

During the childhood years, as boys and girls grow — resulting in longer levers and increased muscle tissue — both have the potential to increase their strength. Boys and girls show similar increased ability to perform motor skills prior to puberty. However, in general, boys are eventually able to develop greater strength and thus surpass girls in the performance of most sport-related skills.

During adolescence males show a steady increase in performance and endurance that extends into early adulthood. The same is not true for girls. There has been a tendency for girls' performance to reach a plateau around the time of puberty (approximately thirteen years of age) and decline thereafter. Because of physical changes that accompany adolescence, such as increases in fat, girls are placed at somewhat of a disadvantage for motor performance. But the leveling off and subsequent decline in girls' performance and endurance have been related more to social factors than to biological changes. Although it is unfortunate, decreased motivation and increased sedentary habits of adolescent females have been prime factors in their lowered performance.

Like other aspects of motor skill, strength shows a steady increase during childhood, with boys being slightly stronger than girls. Boys continue to improve during adolescence, whereas girls' strength scores level off and then tend to decrease. In boys there is a delay, on the average, of at least fourteen months between the period of the most rapid gain in height and the most rapid gain in muscle weight. The young male who is nearing the completion of his rapid adolescent gain in height will have little muscle tissue and strength potential for the next year or two while he awaits the development of muscles to go along with his newly acquired taller body. Because of this lag in strength, the adolescent male is not as strong as his stature might suggest. This was apparent recently in a seven-foot, two-inch basketball freshman at the University of Georgia who had not yet begun his muscle maturation and weight gain. At seven-two he weighed only 172 pounds. When he suffered a muscle strain, his coach remarked, "This is good news and bad news. The bad news is that he is going to miss practice for several days. The good news is that now we know he has a muscle."

Research on strength development of boys under fourteen in training programs is not extensive. The best information available indicates that prior to this age (and the production of the male sex hormone testosterone), weight training cannot be expected to result in any worthwhile gains in either muscle development or strength. In addition, weight training for preadolescent boys is an activity with high injury risk if not rigidly supervised.

Because the increase in weight of the adolescent female is due primarily to a gain in fat (and, to only a small extent, to a gain in muscle), her potential for strength development via exercise is markedly less than the male's. The extent to which girls' smaller amount of muscle tissue can be increased and strength gained by weight training has not been systematically studied. In young adult women, weight training has been shown to produce significant gains in strength, but in the absence of male hormones, the female will experience minimal gains in the size and mass of muscles.

Should Boys and Girls Compete Against Each Other

We have pointed out that during childhood years, only very slight sex differences in body structure and motor performance are present. On a purely physical basis, there is no reason why boys and girls should not be on the same teams competing with and against each other. The potential for performance and the chances for causing or sustaining injury related to size and strength do not differ significantly between the two sexes.

However, this situation changes drastically during adolescence. As boys gain more in height, weight, muscle mass, and strength, it is not possible for girls to fairly and safely compete against them in most sports.

There is little merit to the argument that if a girl is good enough, she should be allowed to compete on the boys' team. If one is to accept this as a valid position, then boys who are good enough should be allowed to play on girls' teams. Boys would occupy most of the places on both teams because of their greater size and strength, and almost all girls would be denied places on either team. After age eleven, boys and girls should have their own competitive opportunities in those sports in which strength and body size are determinants of proficiency and injury risk.

The Growing and Maturing Skeleton

The body skeleton is obviously involved in the normal growth of children. In adolescents the skeleton first grows in size and length, after which it gains in density and strength. As mentioned earlier, the principal sites of growth before the onset of rapid adolescent growth are in the legs and arms. During the adolescent growth spurt, the trunk grows most rapidly. The long bones of the arms and legs increase their length by the activity of highly specialized cells located in a so-called growth plate at either end of the shaft of the long bones.

Because it is composed of cartilage (soft tissue), the growth plate is structurally the weakest point in the bone. It is weaker than any point in the shaft of the bone and actually weaker than the ligaments that align the neighboring joints. Additionally, the growth plate is weakest during periods of most rapid growth. Injury to this area of the bone can destroy those cells responsible for the future growth of the long bone. During the period of the most rapid gain in height (on the average, ages fourteen to fifteen in boys and twelve to thirteen in girls), severe injury to the ends of long bones can threaten the growth plate. Growth arrest and a shortened leg could result in lifelong crippling if a long bone of the leg is involved.

Fortunately, growth-plate injuries are not common in sports. But the threat of a growth-plate injury would temporarily direct rapidly growing, early adolescents away from participation in collision sports, such as football and wrestling, where severe blows to a leg or arm may be encountered. As growth nears completion in later adolescence, the growth plate ceases its function, fuses firmly with the shaft of the long bone, and is no longer the site of vulnerability that it was during early adolescence.

As the skeleton matures, the bones become denser, stronger, and more able to withstand the trauma of hard use in intensive training. There is little information on the effects on the skeleton of intense, repeated athletic activity during childhood and very early adolescence. In the absence of well-documented research, it is doubtless prudent to follow the recommendations of such concerned organizations as the American Academy of Pediatrics' Sports Medicine Committee, which discourages intense athletic activities, such as long-distance running and weight training, during childhood and until the rapid growth of early adolescence has been completed.

Changing Body Functions That Influence Athletic Performance

In recent years exercise scientists have carried out important research into several body functions related to exercise and sport performance and how these functions change during early life. The body's ability to utilize oxygen for energy production shows a striking increase at essentially the same time that there is the greatest increase in muscle mass. This would indicate that only after age fourteen or fifteen for the average maturing male and thirteen to fourteen for the average female is the body ready to respond to intense endurance or (aerobic) training.

The metabolic activity within muscle cells determines the level of energy that is available for athletes to perform their intense muscle work. Each muscle cell called on to do work must have access to a good blood supply, bringing to it fuels, such as fats and sugars, and oxygen to burn these fuels in the production of energy. In addition, certain enzymes that are working parts of this energy factory must be present. As muscle tissues grow rapidly following the rapid adolescent gain in height, they grow faster than the blood capillaries that provide their blood supply. The decreased concentration of blood capillaries in the newly enlarged muscles reduces the supply of energy fuels and oxygen to the muscle cells. Training programs that involve vigorous and regular use of muscles prompt the growth of blood capillaries and an increase in the concentration of blood capillaries in the exercised muscles.

Enzyme chemists have demonstrated that only after the adolescent's new muscle mass is well established (usually at age fifteen or sixteen) do the enzymes essential in controlling energy production appear in adequate amounts to make it possible to respond well to endurance training.

The ability to deal with the heat generated by the vigorously exercising muscles of the athlete has recently become a concern as young children find themselves in very intense athletic competition and training. Prior to adolescence children produce less sweat for evaporative cooling of their skin surfaces and they transport muscle-generated heat less efficiently, but psychologically they adjust to exercise in warm environments much more rapidly than do postpubescent athletes and adults. This places the young child at greater risk to heat exhaustion and even heat stroke and becomes another aspect of growing up that must be considered in managing sports for young children.

Along with growth in height and weight and changes in the body chemistry that governs energy production, important changes occur in the developing nervous system. Sport skills and how effectively they can be performed are dependent on the speed with which the brain and nervous system can react through their information-processing systems. The speed of these reactions increases as children get older, but does not reach full potential until the young person has progressed well into adolescence. Quickness, coordination, and the readiness with which new skills are acquired all require a degree of maturation of the brain and nervous system that is not present in the young athlete.

The immature nervous system won't support the coordination and quickness of reaction needed for a high-level sport skill. Until the exciting physical changes of adolescent development are well under way, young bodies are more suited to just having fun and becoming acquainted with team play and a variety of sports. While playing, the young athlete may slowly begin to develop some early sport skills.

Sport Participation and Maturity

We have mentioned that body structure and a variety of basic functions that relate to athletic performance undergo striking change during the early years of adolescence as well as a great variation in the age at which individuals experience these changes. Therefore, the age at which children (boys in particular) are physically ready for many types of sport involvement will vary greatly. Youth sport programs present the early adolescent (junior high or middle school–aged person) with opportunities for highly organized sports. It thus becomes important to identify late-maturing and early-maturing individuals if they are to be directed into appropriate sport experiences. The late maturer will have increased risk to injury with his undeveloped muscles and immature skeleton. More importantly, playing with and competing against larger, stronger, and more mature boys, the late maturer will be a less-skilled athlete. He is a prime candidate to drop out at the earliest opportunity.

The considerable variation in the onset of physical development at adolescence raises the question of the appropriateness of collision sports for junior high school and middle school boys. After one junior high school football game, twenty-two players were weighed. They varied in weight from 84 to 212 pounds. Although the players' physical maturity was not scientifically assessed, the range of maturity seemed also to be extremely varied — as much as four or five years' variation in skeletal maturity.

Unless rather elaborate steps are taken to match competitors on the basis of maturity and size in football, wrestling, and ice hockey, it is difficult to justify these sports for middle and junior high school programs. These sports can be a positive experience only for the early-maturing individual, and they can sour the taste of athletic participation for many of the others.

Assessing the Young Athlete's Maturation Level

Maturity is a major determinant of proficiency in athletic endeavors. A precise assessment of maturation can serve as a valuable guide to where a child belongs in sports, what can be expected of the child's body responses to training, and how much additional growth and development Nature has in store for a young, aspiring athlete. Being able to know one's maturation status is particularly important to boys during early adolescent development. Of course, few of the physical signs of early development are apparent to coaches, teachers, or peers. This is in contrast to the early-developing young girl, whose broader hips and fuller breasts are evidence to all that her maturation is well under way.

The following figure shows the changes in adolescent male development. This orderly sequence is followed by all healthy boys. However, the age at which the process begins varies tremendously, as does the rate at which individuals pass through various stages of development. Many adolescents will enjoy a much greater degree of security with their changing bodies if they are informed about this sequence of normal events. Many, wondering what their final height might be, are comforted in knowing that hands and feet are the first body parts to stop growing. As long as the shoe size keeps changing, continued growth in body height can be expected.

The most precise assessment of maturation status during childhood and adolescence is made by analysis of X-rays of the growing and developing skeleton. X-rays of the wrist or knee allow the most accurate assessment of biologic maturity. This is referred to as an individual's bone age, which in the average healthy individual will be very similar to his or her calendar or chronologic age. Because there is a wide range in ages at which individuals begin and proceed with their adolescent development, there will be considerable variation in bone age during normal early adolescence. Obviously, bone X-rays are not a practical way to determine the maturity of those being counseled regarding appropriate sport participation. Researchers concerned with growth and development have created a practical maturity scoring system that relates pubic-hair and genital development to other aspects of adolescent development, that is, growth in height, weight, skeletal maturity, muscle mass, and strength. There are five stages of pubic-hair development that can be readily recognized, scored, and related to specific body changes. Not until the later stages are skeletal maturity and muscle-strength potential sufficient to allow the adolescent male to be competitive in high school football, wrestling, lacrosse, and ice hockey. For the average boy this will be at age fifteen or sixteen, although many reach this stage earlier and many somewhat later. When pubic hair begins to appear on the inner upper thighs, the young male will know when to expect a satisfactory response to endurance and weight training.

Since girls have not commonly been involved in sports that are as dependent on muscle mass and strength, their risk of serious injury has not been as great. Therefore, maturation assessment in the young female athlete has not received as much attention in relation to sport participation. As more and more girls become involved in sport programs, many of them and their parents will be interested in knowing what expectations are appropriate for height attainment, endurance, and strength. The sport scene for the female is rapidly changing the way many girls view the body changes of adolescent growth. In the recent past a girl's height was a concern only if she was unusually tall. The very tall girl often suffered a serious social handicap. This has changed. Recently, when asked how tall she was, a member of a women's basketball team replied, "Only six feet, one inch, darn it."

Growth of pubic hair in the female follows the same patterns as in the male in relation to endurance and strength development.

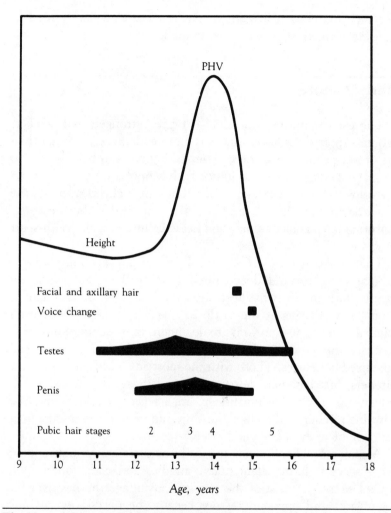

The Normal Sequence of Maturation Changes in the Male during
Adolescence. PHV is Peak Height Velocity, the Most Rapid Period
of Gain in Height.

But such maturation assessment has not been frequently used in advising women about sport participation.

The Early Maturer

The early-maturing individual is bigger, stronger, and quicker, acquires sport skills faster, and has more endurance potential than his or her peers. Thus, the early-maturing boy can be expected to be a star grade school and junior high school athlete. The early-maturing girl until recently was the junior high cheerleader and the first one in her class to be invited to the movies by the early-maturing boy. Today we may find her excelling in some youth-sport program.

That early-maturing boys excel in several juvenile athletic programs has been well documented. In football and track-and-field events, early maturity has been shown to be a prime determinant of proficiency. Players at the Little League World Series have been studied using bone-age X-rays to document their maturation status. Seventy-one percent of these twelve-year-old star athletes had advanced bone ages. Those with the most advanced bone age were pitchers, first basemen, left fielders, and those who batted fourth (clean-up) in the batting lineup. In a recent World Series, the winning pitcher in the championship game was a very mature five-foot, eight-inch, 174-pound twelve-year-old.

A major problem is that the early maturer enjoys outstanding sport success during elementary, middle, and early junior high school simply because of the physical advantages he has over his teammates and opponents—not because he necessarily has any superior sport skills. With the elaborate sport programs available for very young athletes in most communities, the eight- to twelve-year-old can readily become a true sports star. That winning Little League pitcher mentioned above was flown to New York from the West Coast to appear on a national prime-time television show, and he was given a page and a half write-up in *Sports Illustrated*. A local television commentator suggested that the junior high school where he had just started seventh grade be named after him. Pretty heady stuff for a twelve-year-old.

The sport success of an early-maturing boy can lead to a full-time commitment to one or more sports at a very early age. Sport achievements may eliminate the need for accomplishment in other areas, such as schoolwork or the arts, or an interest in exploring other sports. Positive reinforcements come from coaches, teammates, and most particularly parents, who sometimes begin to think of their star athlete in terms of outstanding high school athletic performances, college scholarships, and perhaps even a high-salaried career in professional sports. What does it matter if the only musical instrument the child will ever be interested in playing is a tape deck or that his report card is full of C's and D's?

The world can fall apart for this youngster and his family about high school time, when as a sophomore he lines up against some juniors and seniors who possess his same maturity. Having lost the advantage of his early maturity, the young man is now less than an outstanding athlete. As all of his former grade school teammates and opponents catch up to him in maturity and as other athletes begin to do outstanding things, the grade school star may find only an uncomfortable place on the bench. Unable to understand the true reason that the star no longer outshines others, insensitive coaches and even parents may accuse him of "dogging it." The young man has lost the limelight of sport success on which his self-esteem was built. He is left with no other interests or talents because of his early all-consuming commitment to the sport, and he is keenly aware of the great disappointment he is to his parents. At sixteen or seventeen, an age of considerable vulnerability to a number of disturbing antisocial alternatives, he is a depressed has-been.

The answer, of course, is to prevent the problem from occurring. This can be done by first recognizing the signs of early maturity. The early maturer will probably be the son of a father who likewise was an early maturer, and he will experience the physical changes outlined above well ahead of schedule. Once identified as an individual who is maturing more rapidly than usual, he should have the opportunity to participate in sports with individuals who are of similar maturity, not the same calendar age. The early-maturing star basketball player of junior high school should have a chance to work out with the high school junior varsity. Matches can be arranged for the twelve-year-old tennis star with some sixteen-year-old members at the tennis club. Early-maturing boys need to know how really good they are if they are to keep their athletic performances and potentials in proper perspective.

The Late Maturer

With sport successes so closely related to maturity, it isn't difficult to imagine the problems of the late-maturing boy — especially for parents who were late maturers themselves. Many, but certainly not all, late maturers will be small in stature for their age. All will have less strength, endurance, and skeletal maturity and lower motor skills than their average peers. These boys are going to be handicapped in many sports where size, strength, endurance, and motor skills determine outcome, and in some situations they will be at undue risk to injury.

The late-maturing individual will often be recognized as such in his elementary school years. A father's own maturation experience from twelve to sixteen years of age can be an indicator of the maturation rate to be expected of the son. If early sport participation is important for the late maturer, he should be directed to sports that are not primarily dependent on size and strength for proficiency, such as racket sports, diving, and some track events. He may not become state champion, but he may achieve levels of accomplishment sufficient to earn him a comfortable place in the sport scene.

Many late maturers can comfortably postpone their entry into sport programs until they are physically mature. Club activities, scouting, music, and other activities may satisfy in the meanwhile. It is most important that these boys know the normal sequence of changes that occur during adolescence so that they know where they are in the maturation process, where they are going, and when they get there. With this insight they will know when sports can be rewarding, when a vigorous training program can be effective and satisfying, and when they can be competitive on the field or court. It is possible at ages fourteen to sixteen to avoid a devastating, negative sport experience due to delayed maturity. The late maturer doesn't have to suffer consistent setbacks and be turned off to sports and their benefits.

Special Problems of Certain Late Maturers

Not all late maturers are small. Every high school football team has an aspiring candidate in the fall — a very large, obese, late-maturing sophomore. With no sports skills or talents, he looks to a place in the defensive line. Although large, he has all the handicaps of delayed maturity. He has very little muscle development, an immature skeletal system, a lack of skills, and no endurance potential. He will contribute little to the team, will gain little from the experience, and is at an increased risk to injury, particularly heat disorders during early-season practice.

The obese, late-maturing youngster should be medically disqualified from football. He needs a special training program that includes conditioning and weight control. Once he has corrected his weight problem and become more mature, few things could be more helpful to this youngster than a gratifying sport experience.

Of particular concern these days is the early adolescent who is more than six feet tall when he starts his rapid adolescent growth. He may reach six-eight, six-ten, or even more. He is obviously very attractive to a basketball coach and will himself recognize that basketball is a game that he can become very proficient at. At friendly games at the basket in his driveway, he does very well with his junior high school friends. But when he shows up for the high school team, he is at high risk to some serious disappointments. Arriving at age fifteen or sixteen with all of the "equipment" to be the star of the team—seventy-eight to eighty inches of it—he finds that he has no endurance or strength to hold his own under the boards and that he is slow in picking up new skills. If this young man has just experienced his peak growth in height at age sixteen or is in the midst of it, he is twelve to eighteen months away from his maximum growth in weight and muscle and another year away from gaining strength and endurance. There is no realistic expectation for anything like a satisfying athletic performance from this young athlete until his senior year in high school. And even then his potential as a good athlete will be a few years in the future. In addition to all of the handicaps of the small-statured late maturer, these very tall ones have the height to be athletes but have to live with expectations of coaches and parents that they should perform up to their size—a frustrating impossibility.

Late maturers, in particular, should know the normal growth and development process of adolescents, where they are in the process, and what to expect of their bodies. Coaches and parents should know the implications of delayed adolescent development in these boys, and they should develop their expectations accordingly. Limited training for strength and endurance during the first two years of high school should be accompanied by large doses of encouragement at home and on the court or field. Properly managed, the late maturer can be a budding sport star by the senior year of high school. Being constantly yelled at by a coach or put down by a disappointed parent can produce a devastated dropout at an age when dropping out can be very serious.

A Final Word

The young athlete's body is the prime determinant of proficiency and satisfaction in sport. Since that critical determinant is constantly changing during childhood and adolescence, sports programs and expectations must be adjusted according to these developmental changes. From a purely physical viewpoint, the sport programs of the elementary school–aged preadolescent must minimize demands for strength and endurance. The potential for developing these attributes is not present at this age. Prior to the age of twelve or thirteen, sports should be for fun, for experiencing a variety of sport opportunities, and for being introduced to some sport skills.

During those rapidly changing years from twelve to sixteen, with their tremendous variation in adolescent body changes and with the rate at which they are experienced, an increasing level of attention should be paid to the proper matching of competitors, who should be of a similar maturational level regardless of their calendar ages. Sports provide a critical opportunity to acquire much-needed confidence in oneself and in one's newly developed physique. The adolescent should not be denied this opportunity or have a negative experience because of inappropriate matching or the unrealistic expectations of parents and coaches.

4

Choosing a Sport Program

A First Step to a Good Experience

Betty had a lot of potential. She was tall, strong, and well coordinated for her age. She also had a strong competitive spirit and a genuine interest in gymnastics. But that's all gone now.

Because of Betty's interest in gymnastics, her parents enrolled her in an athletic club near her home. Although the facility was excellent, the program left a lot to be desired from both a medical and psychological point of view. The coach was a hard-driving man who demanded total dedication from youngsters. "Dedication" was instilled by threats that those who did not develop fast enough would not be entered in meets. Daily practices were pressured and exhausting. There was no time for friends or other activities. Like some of the other gymnasts, Betty was put on a highly restrictive diet without medical consultation. At one point the coach suggested that she take illegal steroids to increase her strength and muscle mass. His constant prodding to attempt more dangerous routines resulted in repeated injuries. After a year in the club, Betty completely burned out. She dropped out of gymnastics and vowed never to have anything to do with the sport again.

Pete's story is different. His mother and father were divorced when he was very young. Because his mother was forced to work, he had little parental guidance. As early as the second grade, Pete began to have conduct problems in school. A few years later he became involved with a youth gang and ended up under arrest for shoplifting. He seemed well on his way to a life of delinquency. Pete's life turned around when his mother enrolled him in the local YMCA, where he came under the influence of a young supervisor who steered him into the Youth Basketball Association League. Here Pete found a constructive outlet for his energies, and he developed a sense of belonging. His mother's work schedule allowed her to attend his games, and he felt great pride in being part of the team. His conduct problems in school disappeared, and he began to apply himself to his schoolwork just as he had to basketball.

Pete's story has a happy ending, whereas Betty's is tragic. One youngster found fulfillment in a sport program. The other was turned off as a result of a bad experience. Their stories illustrate the importance of selecting a good program.

Most children enter sports programs more or less through chance. Often a parent knows relatively little about a program, its philosophy, or the nature of the leadership provided. Typically for most children, entering a program is a matter of doing what one's friends are doing or it is a matter of practical factors, such as its location and availability.

But there is much to be said for parental involvement and guidance at even this first stage of selecting a program. Youngsters can't be expected to critically evaluate a particular program. They need the assistance of their parents. If an appropriate program is selected, many unnecessary difficulties and problems can be avoided. Therefore, we strongly recommend that you take the time and effort to arrive at a well-informed choice.

Your Responsibility As a Parent

Parents have both the right and the responsibility to inquire about *all* activities that their children are involved in, including sports. You should take this responsibility seriously, probing into the nature and the quality of specific sports programs. By so doing, you are not being overly protective or showing a lack of confidence in a program. Rather, you are fulfilling a child-rearing obligation to oversee the welfare of your loved one. It is important that you gather the information necessary to make the decision that is right for you and right for your child.

Inquiries by parents, if made appropriately, should be welcomed by sports-program directors and coaches. They, like you, should have as their major concern the welfare of your child. If your inquiries are not welcomed or even responded to, you have cause for concern about the program.

Deciding Together

Selection of a program should be a joint decision of parent and child. Although you have the final say in the matter, it is important to involve your child in the decision-making process, taking into account very seriously what your child wants to get out of the sport experience. It is a mistake for parents to assume that they know what a child wants without asking him or her. A parent whose goal is for the youngster to excel as an athlete might choose a different program than one who takes into account simply the child's desire to participate with his or her friends. A direct discussion in which you share your own experiences and opinions with your youngster rather than force them on him or her is the best approach.

Because all programs are run by human beings, you should not expect to find a fault-free program. Most have certain flaws, but this does not mean that the entire experience will be a bad one for your child. If you make a commitment to work with, not against, a program, you may be able to help correct any shortcomings.

How Early Should Children Participate?

This is not an easy question to answer. Children differ a great deal in their maturity, their aspirations, and their abilities. For this reason it is impossible to recommend a specific age for participation of all children in all sports. In the final analysis it depends on your child's characteristics, the sport in question, and the nature of the program. Children should not be rushed into organized athletics; they need time to enjoy free play with their friends, for much development occurs in such play. Certainly one important indicator of readiness is the child's own expression of interest in participating. But parents and coaches must fall back on common sense to make a decision in a particular case. The best guide is to know the child, the sport, and the program.

Based on available scientific and medical evidence, and taking into account individual differences in physical and psychological readiness to compete, we recommend the following age guidelines:

Noncontact sports (baseball, swimming, track, tennis)	6–8 years
Contact sports (soccer, basketball, wrestling)	8–10 years
Collision sports (tackle football, hockey)	10–12 years

Which Sports Should Your Child Play?

Again, the answer to this question depends basically on your youngster's interests. There are additional factors to be taken into account, however. Such factors as safety, the benefits of individual versus team sports, and the season of the year may all influence decisions. You may be perfectly happy to have your child play outdoor soccer during warm months, but have health concerns about the same sport during cold winter months.

Parents frequently inquire about the benefits of individual versus team sports. Again, there is no simple answer to this question and no reliable scientific research to help guide decisions. However, one can make some broad and general comparisons. On the whole, team sports provide more opportunities for learning social skills and making friends. There is also more need for cooperation and more stress placed on willingness to sacrifice personal interests for the good of the team. More opportunities exist in team sports to specialize and find a niche suited to personal interests and abilities. A youngster with a poor throwing arm can play first base in baseball, and a big youngster with a poor shooting touch can become a rebounding terror in basketball. On the other hand, a youngster in an individual sport, such as tennis, needs to be able to master all the skills of the sport. Finally, it is often the case that team sports generate more camaraderie, or "we" feelings, than do individual sports. Many youngsters are attracted to the sense of belonging that exists in team sports.

Individual sports generally require more self-sufficiency. The athlete cannot rely on anyone else to get the job done. Competition takes the form of one-on-one duels, and success or failure is shouldered solely by the individual. There is less of the social support that is provided by teammates in team sports. This can foster a strong sense of personal responsibility and independence. Because of these factors, individual sports tend to be more intensely competitive at a personal level and often demand more in the way of "mental toughness." Also, more personal dedication is often required of the athlete in training.

We feel that almost all sports have something to offer children. However, we do have major reservations about boxing. Boxing is the only sport whose goal is to harm another person. Reports of twelve-year-old amateur boxers who have registered strings of knockouts are chilling reminders of the basic brutality of the sport. Although we acknowledge the fact that some underprivileged youths have found social and economic salvation through boxing, we do not believe that boxing in itself offers any youth sport benefits that cannot be achieved through other, less dangerous sports.

How Many Sports Should Your Child Play?

No matter how enjoyable or fulfilling sport participation is, it does take time and divert attention from other activities. For most children one sport at a time is plenty during the school year. The time and energy demands on both children and their parents need to be kept at a reasonable level.

During the summer months multiple-sport participation seems more reasonable. A child may have enough time and energy to be involved in several sports, such as baseball, tennis, and swimming.

Sometimes the best decision is not to participate. Participation in sport, although desirable, is not necessarily for everyone. Parents should not feel that their child must be on a team or involved in a sport. For those children who wish to direct their energies in other ways, the best program may be no program. Many parents become unnecessarily alarmed if their child does not show an interest in sports. They think that a child who would rather do other things must somehow be abnormal. Forcing a child into sports against his or her will can be a big mistake. Sometimes the wisest decision is to encourage the child to move into other activities that may be more suited to his or her interests and abilities, at least until an interest in sports develops.

Sources of Information and How to Get It

Many programs have preseason meetings to provide parents with information and to answer their questions. Such meetings can also serve as forums for parents to give input regarding concerns, opinions, and suggestions. If you attend a meeting of this kind, look for openness on the part of sports administrators and a willingness to exchange information with the intent of promoting greater understanding and cooperation. If a program does not have such a meeting, you might suggest it to the administrator and perhaps volunteer to assist in its organization.

If a preseason meeting is not scheduled for parents, you may have to obtain information directly from the program administrators or coaches. It is well to make up a list of questions and concerns before speaking with them. In dealing with program leaders, it is also well to remember that they are volunteering their time and effort for the benefit of the children who participate in their program. They are deserving of courtesy and respect.

Another very useful source of information about a program is parents of youngsters who have been through it. They can provide firsthand and candid feedback concerning the merits and shortcomings of the program. As consumers of the program, they may be in the best position to evaluate it for you.

Some Important Considerations in Deciding on a Program

Eventually the decision will come down to whether or not to join a particular program. Sometimes you might be choosing among several alternatives, such as the church-sponsored basketball league, the one sponsored by your local parks department, or the one at the junior high. At other times there may be only one program available, and your decision will be based on whether it meets your child's needs and whether the costs or possible physical risks involved are balanced by the benefits. In either of these cases, there are some key points about sports programs that you should keep in mind to help guide your decision.

Organization and Administration

The success of any program depends on how it is run and who is running it. You should make it a point to find out whether the program is administered by one person or by a board of directors (which is likely to include a wider range of viewpoints and representation). Of crucial importance is the extent to which you as a parent can have an influence on decisions that will affect your child. Potential problems can occur when a program is run by a small clique that is not open to input from you, the consumer of the program. Programs also vary in how much information they give parents about policies and practices. Parents should be given an account of how revenues are spent to benefit children. Two key questions to ask are whether board meetings are held and if parents are welcome to attend. Some very effective programs welcome involvement by parents in a variety of ways and organize social events in which parents can interact with their children.

Costs and Commitments

It's rare in this world to get something for nothing. Most programs require commitments of time and money. It's wise for parents to know the costs sooner rather than later. The costs can be financial — entry fees, equipment, uniforms, transportation for trips, contributions to fund raisers, and so forth. In sports such as tennis, gymnastics, and figure skating, these costs can multiply rapidly in the form of private lessons and coaching, racket- or skating-club fees, and trips to distant meets. Many parents have found themselves in over their heads financially and unable to pull back because the child has become involved beyond the point of return. It's a good idea to ask parents who are already in the program for information.

Other costs may be in terms of time and emotional involvement. You can easily get into a program for your child's sake (or for your own hoped-for peace and quiet), only to find yourself mired in a quicksand of time commitments. Suddenly you're spending hours driving to games and practices, manning the hot dog booth, and going door-to-door selling candy bars. Those glorious days of working in the garden or watching the weekend ball games on TV are now a thing of the past.

Now, you may well make the choice to be time-involved, but to make an informed decision, you should try to find out

- How many practices and games per week are there? Where are they held? Who provides transportation? Is there car pooling?

- What responsibilities are expected of parents? For example, are they expected to organize fund raisers or to participate in field maintenance?

- Are allowances made for family vacations during the season, or will your family's vacation have to be postponed or canceled?

- Will your child have time for other activities? Obviously, if practices are held every night for two hours, there will be little time for other pursuits.

- Do practices and game schedules interfere with dinner time, homework, church or Sunday school, or family outings?

- How long does the season last? In warm climates youth baseball tryouts can begin as early as January, making for a far longer season than in snowbound regions.

Program Philosophy and Objectives

The philosophy and values underlying a program can mean the difference between a positive experience and a negative one for your child. These values influence the goals that are set and the approaches used to pursue them.

In Chapter 1 we stressed the crucial differences between the professional model and the developmental model of sports. It is important to keep these differences in mind as you examine a program. To put it briefly, the professional model operates on the premise that winning is everything, whereas the developmental model insists that kids are everything.

Although we believe that the psychological and physical welfare of child athletes is best served in programs that emphasize participation, fun, and personal growth, we also recognize that some parents and children prefer win-oriented programs, even at very early ages. At the high school level, virtually all programs emphasize athletic excellence and winning. It is a parent's right to choose such a program, but it is also the parent's responsibility to make sure that winning is not emphasized to the exclusion of the young athlete's interests. Many cases of athletic burnout result from pressures created by program philosophies that place winning first and athletes second.

Some national programs emphasize their underlying philosophy very directly. Little League Baseball, the American Youth Soccer Association, the YWCA and YMCA, the Catholic Youth Organization, the American Junior Bowling Congress, and the United States Wrestling Federation are among those whose philosophies emphasize personal growth through sports. However, at a local level even these programs can vary in their commitment to the principles of the larger organization. Therefore, it is important to examine each program on an individual basis and to talk with parents whose children have been in the programs.

In examining a particular program, you may wish to get answers to the following questions:

- Does the program have a written statement of its goals and philosophy that is available to parents? If so, are they consistent with your needs?

- Is participation for everyone emphasized? Do all youngsters who turn out get a chance to play? Do some players get cut? Are there rules requiring that all children on a team get a certain amount of playing time?

- Is competition kept in perspective? Is competition seen as deadly serious business or as a contest in which to have fun? Are players taught to regard their opponents as enemies or as friendly challengers who make the contest possible?

- Are the needs of athletes taken into account in making decisions about such things as the time and length of practices and games? Are there attempts to match teams on the basis of size and ability for safe and equal competition?

- Are youngsters treated fairly? Do all children receive attention and instruction, or only the best performers? Is the emphasis on giving every child a good experience or on developing a select group of gifted athletes for higher levels of competition?

- Are attempts made to teach children sportsmanship and moral values? Is social and emotional development promoted?

- Are the rewards of participation viewed in terms of personal and team improvement or in the form of trophies, victory banquets, and all-star teams? Is the most improved player as important to the program as the most valuable player?

Program Safety

The physical well-being of your youngster is surely of concern in choosing a program. There will always be injuries in sports, but a safety-conscious program can help keep the risks at a minimum.

Many programs are emphasizing the desirability of a medical examination prior to participating, and some programs are requiring it. Children who have a physical condition that places them at high risk can often be identified and saved from injury. Several medical studies have shown preparticipation physical examinations to be associated with a lower rate of serious injuries.

Recognizing the value of screening examinations, some programs have contracted with sports medicine clinics or with individual physicians to make the exams less costly for parents. It is wise to inquire about this when selecting a program.

The safety of participants is increased when a program has developed safety rules for practices and games and when such rules are strictly enforced. Playing areas should be kept safe and free from hazards, such as holes, rocks, and broken glass. Your inquiry into these matters helps to draw necessary attention to them.

Try as we might to prevent them, injuries will occur and occasionally they will be serious ones. It is therefore important that coaches or adult supervisors who are trained in first aid be present at practices and games. There should also be established procedures in the event of an emergency. Safety-conscious programs have leaders who are prepared to deal quickly and effectively with injuries and emergencies when they occur.

Everyone is aware of the rising costs of health care and the resulting need to have insurance protection. Some programs require accident insurance for all participants. Several insurance groups offer athletic accident insurance to youth sport programs at reasonable rates. You should inquire about such coverage when considering a program. If the program does not subscribe to injury insurance, be certain that your own insurance provides adequate coverage for sports-related injuries to your youngster.

The likelihood of injuries increases when participants vary greatly in size, strength, and maturity. It is the smaller, less-developed player who is at greater risk under such circumstances. Research has shown that injuries can be reduced in collision sports, such as football or hockey, by matching participants in terms of size rather than by relying simply on age. Such matching not only reduces injuries but also gives all participants a greater opportunity to enjoy success and fair competition.

Quality of Leadership

When all is said and done, the most important factor of all in determining the outcome of your child's experience is the quality of adult supervision in the program you choose. The relationship that develops between your youngster and the coach or manager can become a very important one in your child's life. This adult will not only teach your child the techniques of the sport, but will also create a psychological climate that can have long-term effects. Coaches communicate important attitudes and values, and they serve as role models for children at an impressionable time in their lives.

Anytime you place your child in the hands of another adult, you should have confidence that he or she has what it takes to shoulder the responsibilities. Remember, most youth sport programs are staffed by volunteers who are sincerely interested in children. But this interest must be accompanied by knowledge of the sport and of a child's needs. The most effective coaches are not only good teachers but good amateur psychologists as well.

Many programs now recognize that they have a responsibility to prepare coaches for their leadership role. They also realize that instruction in the technical aspects of the sport is not enough. Workshops and clinics should focus on how to create a good psychological environment for personal and social growth and how to promote the physical safety of participants. Selection of a program for your youngster should thus be based in part on how well coaches are trained and evaluated. No matter what the program's potential may be, a subpar coach can ruin an otherwise good experience.

Before the season begins and while you're looking into a program, you may not know much about who will be coaching your youngster. At this point about all you can do is to ask whether the coaches have preseason training or have gone through a certification program. Once the season begins, however, you will have opportunities to observe the coach. This is your right and your responsibility.

What should you look for in a coach? Here is a short checklist of qualities that we believe are important in a youth sport coach.

Knowledge and Teaching Skills

- Does the coach know the rules and techniques of the sport? Can he communicate these to children?

- Does she demonstrate how to perform and give clear explanations?

- Are practices and games well organized, safe, and fun for the children?

- Is instruction matched to the age and knowledge level of the children? Or is the coach creating a Dallas Cowboy multiple offense out of his team of eight-year-olds, who are probably not yet certain whether the face mask faces front or back?

Motives and Philosophy

- Does the coach seem to have a sincere interest in youngsters, or is coaching an ego trip?
- Does she put winning and losing in perspective? Is the focus where it should be — on fun, participation for all, and learning?
- Does the coach teach values as well as skills?
- Can she communicate her coaching philosophy to players and parents?

Coaching Style

- Does the coach try to motivate players through encouragement and praise, or do punishment and criticism dominate?
- Does the coach seem enthusiastic and enjoy relating to his players? Does he have fun?
- Are substitutes given as much attention as the stars, or are they ignored and made to feel unimportant?
- Does the coach keep things well organized and prevent misbehavior, or does he let things get out of hand and have to scold the children to maintain control?
- Does the coach recognize and praise good effort even when things are not going well?
- Does the coach ask for input from players and listen to it, or does she call all the shots?
- Can the coach control his own emotions, or does he lose his cool with players or officials and provide a poor role model?

Relationship Skills

- Is the coach sensitive to the individual needs and feelings of her athletes?
- Can he be flexible and know when everybody should *not* be treated exactly alike?
- Can she generate respect without demanding it and show respect for her players, officials, and opponents?
- Is he fair and consistent in his expectations of players?
- Can she communicate effectively with youngsters at their level?

- Do players she has coached wish to play for her again?
- Does he take the time and effort to communicate with parents, and is he open to their input?

Obviously no sport program is going to be perfect, since all are run by fallible human beings. You can't expect to get answers to every question presented here. But weighing the pros and cons can help you increase the chances of selecting the best program for your youngster and starting your young athlete on the road to a good sport experience.

5

Conditioning

Shaping Up for Competition

Conditioning, or getting in shape, is as much a part of sport as the competition itself. Today's recreational athlete is becoming increasingly concerned with good conditioning practices simply to stay fit, feel better, and enjoy his or her hours of sport. For the young athlete a proper introduction to the need for and the techniques of good conditioning is essential to a good beginning.

At the turn of the century, world-class swimmers, champions in the modern Olympic Games, trained and conditioned with two twenty-minute swims each day — twenty minutes in the water in the morning and another twenty-minute workout in the afternoon. In the eyes of today's young swim champions, such a training schedule borders on the ridiculous, since modern training involves swimming 15,000 to 20,000 meters (nine to twelve miles) a day, plus vigorous conditioning exercises outside the pool.

Today's swimmers and other athletes are establishing new world records every year by taking advantage of conditioning methods developed in modern exercise-science laboratories. Scientists have developed practical measures of fitness and have identified components of effective conditioning programs. Such conditioning programs are useful not only for the world-class swimmer and elite athlete preparing for competition but also for the casual recreational athlete or the individual who simply wants to take care of his or her body and enjoy feeling fit. A proper conditioning program, an essential part of the education of every young girl or boy, not only is necessary to enjoying sports, it is a keystone in lifelong fitness and good health.

Exercise scientists have identified five components of a comprehensive conditioning program. These are body composition, flexibility, strength and power, endurance, and speed.

Body Composition

Certain levels of body fatness are associated with elite performance in various popular sports, with certain positions on some teams, and with different events in track and field. Body fatness can be estimated by measuring skin fat folds. The result is expressed as the percentage of body weight that is estimated to be made up of body fat.

The levels of fatness listed in the accompanying table provide general goals for early preseason conditioning. Commonly, it is necessary to reduce body fat to the desired level. The fatness levels

**Relative Body-Fat Values for Male and Female Athletes
in Various Sports***

Sport	Males	Females
	Fat (%)	Fat (%)
Baseball/softball	12–14	16–26
Basketball	7–10	16–27
Football	8–18	—
Gymnastics	4–6	9–15
Ice hockey	13–15	—
Jockeys	12–15	—
Skiing	7–14	18–20
Soccer	9–12	—
Speed skating	10–12	—
Swimming	5–10	14–26
Track and field		
Sprinters	6–9	8–20
Middle distance runners	6–12	8–16
Distance runners	4–8	6–12
Discus	14–18	16–24
Shot put	14–18	20–30
Jumpers and hurdlers	6–9	8–16
Tennis	14–16	18–22
Volleyball	8–14	16–26
Weight lifting	8–16	—
Wrestling	4–12	—

*The values represent the range of means reported in various published and unpublished studies.

listed in the table are for elite athletes and are compatible with the finest levels of health and fitness — when these levels are reached in a proper manner. In the chapter dealing with nutrition, there are directions for a program of fatness reduction compatible with good health and effective training. But the essential points are worth repeating: Allow plenty of time to reduce body fat. Decrease body-fat weight at a rate no more rapid than two to three pounds each week. Calculate a specific goal of fatness level and determine what the body weight will be when that fatness level is achieved. This weight should be the athlete's stable competing weight, which should be constant throughout the sports season.

Reducing body fat demands increasing training, which requires the expenditure of a significant amount of energy. In addition, a modest reduction in food intake is essential during the period of fatness reduction. The diet during this period of early preseason conditioning should be no less than approximately 2,000 kilocalories per day for a typical high school or college-aged athlete.

For the junior high school male who wishes to control his level of fatness for sports participation, his energy intake should also be no less than 2,000 kilocalories, if growth is to continue at a normal weight. For many chubby but rapidly growing junior high school students who are just beginning to play sports seriously, it is often a good policy to maintain a stationary weight through a program of conditioning exercises and a controlled diet while they continue their rapid growth and outgrow their moderate fatness. Modest increases in body fat normally occur in boys immediately before they experience the rapid linear growth of early adolescence. This is merely Nature's way of providing some stored energy in anticipation of the great nutrition demands of adolescent growth. It is a normal increase in fat and is not an indication that one is to live with a fat, clumsy klutz of an adolescent during junior and senior high school years.

It is helpful in every conditioning program to make a decision as to the goals of the program and how intensely involved a given individual will become in it. The highly competitive scholastic or collegiate athlete will be satisfied with nothing less than the ideal body composition for a particular sport. The young preadolescent on the soccer team, for example, may make less of a commitment to fitness. Conditioning for such young athletes may be confined to regular energy-expending exercise, a good mixed diet, and enjoyable, regular sport participation. Their goal should be to maintain a normal body fatness level of 12 to 14 percent rather than the very trim 6 to 8 percent of the elite population of professional soccer players.

Paying attention to fatness level is a sound part of the conditioning program of all individuals regardless of sex or age. Exercise involving regular expenditures of energy is the first essential to fatness control for everyone, including the obese preadolescent. At this age, the fat level is controlled for health and fitness, not to develop elite athletic skills in some sport. Maintaining a desired body composition should also be seen by the ten- to twelve-year-old girl or boy as important to health and fitness — not just to make him or her a better athlete.

An early conditioning program has the potential to alter body composition by increasing body muscle mass. Large numbers of adolescent males are interested in increasing their body weight to improve their playing potential in high school or community-based sports programs. American football is an obvious example of a very popular sport that gives a premium in performance to heavier, stronger individuals. Many young men attempt to increase their body weight by eating more to become more proficient football players. As pointed out in the nutrition chapter, only muscle work will increase muscle weight and size, and this will occur to any great extent only in a healthy male *after* the onset of pubertal hormonal changes — after age fifteen or sixteen on the average. Thus the young man who wants to increase his playing potential by increasing his muscle weight will have to become involved in a regular weight-training program. (Muscle work by women will generally only increase their strength, not their muscle weight or size.) In addition the young man should record all the food eaten in a weight-maintenance diet so that he can document a daily increase of 700 to 800 kilocalories of any preferred foods. Here again, planning ahead is essential. The maximum weight gain in lean body tissues — muscle — is about one to two pounds per week. The weight-training portion of any conditioning program should be carefully supervised. It should involve all of the body's large muscle groups.

For females, both before and after the onset of puberty, weight training and increased food intake will have little effect in increasing muscle weight. Women who are well into the changes of adolescence or older will experience some increase in muscle strength from a weight-training program. There is too little information available at the present time to estimate how great an increase in muscle weight might occur in a well-planned weight-training program. But it will be much less than in the male, even with the same effort. No doubt there will be considerable individual variation in the response of young women to weight-training.

Achieving and controlling a desired body composition through a well-planned preseason conditioning program can provide one of the greatest health benefits of athletic participation.

Flexibility

The serious young athlete and the active recreational-sport participant will both benefit from developing joint flexibility and fluidity of motion. Good flexibility may reduce some of the risk of muscle and tendon injuries in vigorous exercise and competition. It can reduce soreness and stiffness after exercise, and it is conducive to that fluidity of motion that is seen in very talented and so-called natural athletes. Stretching exercises and improved joint mobility are important for all athletes, but participants in some sports are more dependent on good flexibility than others. The high hurdler must have a high degree of flexibility, the swimmer must have well-developed ankle and shoulder flexibility, and those in various running events in track competition receive particular benefit from flexibility exercises, since they may develop very tight muscles from the tremendous amount of running during their training. Flexibility may decrease the risk of injury and it does improve performance.

Muscles can be stretched and flexibility gained in one of two ways: by bouncing or jerking stretches, or by holding a muscle in a stretched position for several seconds. The following are static flexibility exercises that stretch each of the major muscle groups. These maneuvers provide a good general stretching program. Certain sports and the use of specific muscle groups may demand stretching other specific muscle groups.

In the exercises that follow, static stretching is done by slowly lengthening the muscle until the first signs of real pull, or tightness. The position is held for five to ten seconds. Then the stretch is slowly released as one assumes the original starting position. It is ill-advised to bounce, jerk, or painfully force the stretch. Tightness, soreness, and small muscle tears can result, and these are counter-productive to the goals of fluidity and flexibility of motion that one is trying to achieve. A good flexibility-maintenance routine is the following, to which stretches for a particular sport can be added.

> **Trunk rotation.** With hands on the hips and the feet shoulder width apart, twist to the left as far as possible and then twist to the right as far as you can.
>
> **Shoulder rotation.** Extend one arm and rotate it completely around in the largest possible circle. Do each arm separately, first forward and then in the opposite direction.
>
> **Side stretch.** Spread the feet about three feet apart, put your hands behind your head, and keep your legs straight. Now lean sideways until you begin to feel the muscles pull along the side of the trunk.

Hamstring stretch. With the feet together and the legs straight at the knee, lean forward until you feel, in the large muscles in the back of the upper leg, a sensation of pulling. Hold the position for five to ten seconds, and repeat.

Quadriceps stretch. Grasp your right foot behind your body as you hold on to the edge of a table or chair for balance. Pull the right foot up toward the back of your body until you feel a pull in the large muscle mass in the front of the thigh. Hold the position for five seconds, and return to a standing position with both feet on the ground. Repeat the stretching procedure with the left foot and left hand, stretching the left quadriceps muscle mass on the front of the left thigh.

Calf-muscle stretch. With the left foot about three feet behind the right foot, both feet facing forward and flat on the ground, bend the right knee and lean forward, keeping the left heel flat on the ground. You will begin to feel a pull in the muscles in the back of the lower leg, the calf muscles. Hold the position for five seconds. Repeat with the feet reversed, stretching the calf muscles of the opposite lower leg.

For the active recreational athlete or the younger competitor in junior or senior high school, each of these stretching maneuvers is best repeated ten to twelve times. Conscientious athletes will stretch out with this routine before *and* after each practice. Many trainers and experienced athletes firmly believe that a well-followed stretching program is important in the prevention of sports injuries. The scientific sport medicine literature does not provide evidence to support such a statement, but good stretching will increase motion and performance and make active participation more pleasurable, even for the very young athlete.

Strength and Power

There are few sports in which performance cannot be related to strength. The football player, the wrestler, the oarsman, the soccer player and the basketball player all become more competitive when they develop their muscle strength and power through appropriate conditioning practices. Thus, strength-training programs are a very real part of training for almost all serious athletes. It wasn't long ago when many coaches and elite athletes feared that strength training and conditioning would make the athlete muscle-bound, with limited motion, speed, and flexibility. Scientific investigation has shown that quite the opposite is true. Proper strength training actually increases flexibility and enhances speed while increasing strength and power at the same time.

Evidence of strength in sport is readily apparent to any sport observer. The football lineman who essentially picks up the 225-pound blocking back and sets him neatly out of the play is demonstrating pure strength. Muscle power, on the other hand, is the explosive strength that is applied in the briefest time period: the fraction of a second when the shot put is hurled to a new record; when the baseball pitcher puts extra speed on his fastball; or when the high jumper goes over the bar.

In addition to muscle power and muscle strength, there is a factor of muscle endurance that is influenced by conditioning and that becomes a determinant of muscle performance. The young wrestler who may be quick and strong and powerful may not do well against an opponent with less strength and power if his muscle endurance is not as great. Even in the racket sports, such as tennis, squash, and paddleball, the arm strength required to hit the ball well may not always be as important as the muscle endurance needed in long matches, in which hundreds of power-demanding shots can wear out the arm.

The techniques used to condition muscles for strength, power, and endurance can vary greatly. Following is a muscle-conditioning program for strength development that can be implemented without any special muscle-training apparatus or weight-training facilities. As a home-based, gadget-free program, it can very effectively condition the major muscle groups for strength and endurance when pursued regularly. This simple but effective strengthening program is compatible with the proper sports goals of anyone at any age with any reasonable commitment to sports.

1. **Sit-up.** Lying on the back with the knees bent, keeping the lower back flat against the floor and the hands behind the head, curl forward, feeling the pull on the abdominal muscles. (In the past it was common to stabilize the feet under a piece of furniture or to have a partner hold them in place. This is ill-advised because it brings into play muscles other than those of the abdominal wall and it negates the intended benefit of the exercise.) You can add effectiveness by lying in front of a chair or a bed, resting your lower legs on the upper surface as you do the exercise.

2. **Push-up.** This conventional, well-known exercise is a good one. Be sure to keep the legs straight and the fingers pointing forward while lowering the upper chest down to the ground and returning to the starting position.

3. **Stationary jump.** Leg strength and jumping ability can be improved by repeatedly doing the standing jump. From a standing position, simply swing the arms upward and jump as high as possible. Repeat.

4. **Pull-up.** Grasp a bar with the knuckles facing you, and slowly pull the body up until the chin is over the bar. Be sure not to jerk or twist the legs. Return slowly to the original hanging position. Females who have less upper-body muscle strength can substitute fifteen seconds of hanging from the bar for one pull-up.

5. **Hill run.** Using either a steep hill in the neighborhood or the rows of seats at the school gym or grandstand, run at top speed up the incline for five seconds. Return to the starting position and repeat.

William Haskell, distinguished exercise scientist from Stanford University and the proponent of this highly effective and simple strength-conditioning program, recommends a progression of the above numbered exercises (see the table below) in a conditioning program for males and females. For the more committed high school athlete who is involved in a specific sport, there are special supplementary exercises to strengthen specific muscle groups.

A word about strength training with weight apparatus: In almost every high school and certainly in every metropolitan community, there are weight-lifting gyms with strength-conditioning programs that involve the use of elaborate and often very expensive equipment. Effective as these machines are, if used improperly they can be dangerous and harmful, particularly to the young athlete. The results of a good weight-training program depend not on any machine but on the athlete and the effort that he or she can muster to put into the program. If weight-training machines are to be used, young athletes should use them only under competent, professional supervision. Also, they will avoid many of the risks of injury if they stay with the program regularly. Irregular, spotty participation is the surest road to injury and poor results. Finally, weights and weight-training machines were made for adult males. The machines

Schedule for Strength-Training Program for Females

Progression	Number of Repetitions				
	Exercise 1	*Exercise 2*	*Exercise 3*	*Exercise 4*	*Exercise 5*
Level 1	1	5	9	1	4
Level 2	2	8	10	1	4
Level 3	3	11	10	1	5
Level 4	4	12	12	2	5
Level 5	5	13	13	2	6
Level 6	6	14	14	3	6
Level 7	7	15	15	3	7

Schedule for Strength-Training Program for Males

Progression	Number of Repetitions				
	Exercise 1	*Exercise 2*	*Exercise 3*	*Exercise 4*	*Exercise 5*
Level 1	10	10	9	4	4
Level 2	15	15	10	5	4
Level 3	19	19	11	6	5
Level 4	22	22	12	7	5
Level 5	25	25	13	8	6
Level 6	28	28	14	9	6
Level 7	30	30	15	10	7

don't fit children, most adolescents, and females. This adds to the risk of injury. Use them only with supervision and the guidance of a knowledgeable weight coach.

A set of free weights at home can be excellent conditioning aids for noncompetitive adults to use in keeping fit. They can be very dangerous toys for children, however. The preadolescent who wishes to go downstairs and lift with Dad or an older brother should never pick up anything he or she can't comfortably lift seven times and should never lift weights above the head. Most importantly the preadolescent should never use weights in the absence of a supervising adult.

Endurance

The strength-training program that we have just discussed will increase the number of times a muscle group can work without becoming fatigued. For example, the number of pull-ups the young athlete can do will increase with each step in his or her strength training. The endurance that the athlete must have to sustain effort such as running, swimming, or cycling is quite a different kind of endurance. It is dependent on how efficiently the athlete can extract oxygen from the air by breathing and transporting it through the cardiovascular system to the working muscles. Those sports that demand endurance of this type, that use sustained muscle action for a minute or more, are called aerobic (oxygen-dependent) sports. The athlete's ability to extract oxygen from the air and transport it to the muscles is known as his or her aerobic capacity, and the limits of this capacity vary among individuals.

Potential aerobic capacity is an inherited trait. Training will improve almost everyone's aerobic capacity, that is, the ability to utilize oxygen to produce muscle energy, but only to the degree determined by genes. The world-class sprinter will never be a world-class distance runner. His or her world-class energy mechanisms and muscle power for running sprints won't provide the strength and endurance needed in the distance run. The elite sprinter wasn't born to be an elite distance runner.

The capacity to use oxygen for muscle work — the aerobic capacity of the athlete — is commonly measured in the laboratory by actually measuring the amount of oxygen that is inhaled during a strenuous exercise test. Measuring how much is inhaled and how much is exhaled allows scientists to calculate the precise ability of the individual to use oxygen in energy production. By repeating such tests, researchers can document the progressive improvement in aerobic capacity that results from a training program. With a regular program of intense training, progress can be impressive, but sooner or later things reach a point where no further increases are seen. The genetically controlled limit for oxygen utilization has been reached.

To train for increases in aerobic capacity, or the endurance needed for moderate to long efforts, coaches use moderate-intensity exercises, such as distance running, prolonged swimming, or bicycle riding, over a long time period. More recently, exercise scientists, such as the late Edward Fox at Ohio State University, have demonstrated that short stints of moderate- to high-intensity exercise are highly effective in increasing aerobic capacity. Such training exercises are usually more attractive to and efficient in the training schedules of most athletes. Athletes now practice repeated three- to five-minute bouts of exercise to generate heart rates that indicate they are working at 80 to 90 percent of their aerobic capacity. Reaching this level of effort may require a young athlete to train regularly four or more days a week for six weeks or more.

To determine how close to maximum aerobic capacity one is exercising and how much potential for increase there may be with further training, you may simply monitor heart rates during exercises. The heart rate is a valid indicator of aerobic capacity and of how close to maximum the body is working to use oxygen. The interested young scholastic athlete can determine his or her maximum heart rate during intense exercise, and because heart rate and oxygen uptake correspond so closely, knowing one gives us a reliable measure of the other. To determine maximum heart rate you will need a wristwatch with a sweep-second hand.

1. Stretch and warm up very well.

2. Run at a speed that you can continue for only two or three minutes.

3. When you can't go any farther, slow down and count your pulse rate for ten seconds. Counting the pulse can be most easily done using the large vessels and pulse deep in front of the neck. You will want to practice taking your pulse before your trial run. Repeat the maximal-pulse running test a few times on different days until you get a reasonably consistent result. This number of pulse beats multiplied by six will be your maximal heart rate. Pulse rate will vary in individuals during their teenaged years from a high of 210 per minute to no more than 175 or 180.

An effective conditioning program to improve aerobic capacity involves exercising at progressively greater levels of maximum aerobic capacity for relatively brief periods of time and performing such exercise repeatedly. Begin with a limited number of exercise bouts at 60 to 70 percent of maximum aerobic capacity, as measured by your pulse rate. Increase the number of exercise bouts and the level of intensity up to 80 or 90 percent of maximum pulse rate. Your aerobic capacity will become conditioned to your inherited level of maximum ability to use oxygen. William Haskell has provided the accompanying table to determine from the ten-second pulse rate the percentage of maximum aerobic capacity that different exercises produce. A progressive exercise schedule based on the concept of interval training is outlined in the following table. Doing the exercises three or four times each week will result in progressive improvement in aerobic capacity, and two or three aerobic workouts each week will be enough to generally maintain a given level.

Ten-Second Heart Rates: Percentage of Maximum

Maximum Heart Rate

Beats per Minute		Beats per 10 Seconds	
204–209	25–27	27–29	29–31
198–203	24–26	26–28	28–30
192–197	23–25	25–27	27–29
186–191	23–24	24–25	25–26
180–185	22–23	23–24	24–25
% Maximum	60–70%	70–80%	80–90%

Aerobic Training Schedule, Running or Swimming

Level	Work Description	Repetitions	Intensity	Total Time
Aerobic I	5 min. work, 5 min. recovery*	3	60–70%	30 min.
Aerobic II	5 min. work, 5 min. recovery	4	60–70%	40 min.
Aerobic III	4.5 min. work, 5 min. recovery	4	70–80%	38 min.
Aerobic IV	4 min. work, 4 min. recovery	5	70–80%	40 min.
Aerobic V	3.5 min. work, 4 min. recovery	5	80–90%	38 min.
Aerobic VI	3 min. work, 3 min. recovery	6	80–90%	36 min.

*During recovery period, you should not totally rest, but continue to exercise at an easy intensity (walk slowly, cycle slowly, hang on pool edge and tread slowly, and so on).

Speed

Speed and quickness are critical talents of the high-performing athlete in almost all sports. In large part speed and quickness are talents that athletes are born with and can't be taught or trained for. It is not surprising that these attributes are at the top of the list of things looked for by college and professional sports-talent scouts. Good coaching can teach the coachable athlete to throw, slide, bat, serve, block, or pass, but no one can be taught to be fast and quick.

There are, however, some things that can be done to improve the efficiency of fast movements, even for the athlete who wasn't born quick, with fast-reacting muscles. Thus, speed training becomes the fifth part of a good conditioning program.

Each of the preceding four conditioning procedures makes a contribution to speed. Muscle strength contributes, particularly in the first few yards of acceleration. Good stretching programs that increase flexibility, fluidity of motion, and efficiency of body movements make small but helpful contributions to speed. Running short distances at speeds greater than are needed in the sport can condition for speed. Most important for the athlete who is not endowed with outstanding speed are so-called specialty exercises that simulate competitive situations encountered in a particular sport. For example, the baseball player practices all-out base running with a quick slide at the end of the circuit. The basketball player repeatedly practices full-court speed dribbling with a lay-up at the end of the court. The soccer player plays one-on-one the full length of the field, setting up a goal shot at the end of the field.

Such drills have a small but somewhat helpful effect on the quickness of muscle response. In addition, they have a very real functional impact as they prompt the athlete to develop good anticipation, a trait that pays off well in games.

Some Basics in Conditioning Programs

Response and effectiveness are determined by the attention that is given to certain basic principles operating in all conditioning efforts. These principles include individuality, overload, progression, and specificity.

Individuality

Nowhere is the principle of individuality in conditioning more critical than with very young and new athletes. The response to any conditioning effort will vary greatly among all of us. Potentials for strength, quickness, coordination, intensity of effort, and interest all vary among individuals and all influence the conditioning response of adults. Most adults will have, through past experience with muscle work, a pretty good idea of just what kind of training response to expect in comparison to others. In the instance of young and new athletes, there is no basis of previous experience to tell them whether they will make rapid progress through the progressive steps of the strength or endurance conditioning chart or whether they are destined to take an extra week at one or more steps before they can move ahead. Nor do they know as yet how far in any conditioning activity their bodies are going to be able to go. These potentials of performance, inherited and genetically determined, have not been tested as yet. It is important for parents and coaches of very young athletes to be understanding and reassuring during these explorations of physical conditioning.

Overload

The key to maximizing response to conditioning is the principle of overload — regularly increasing the intensity of the conditioning effort. The increase may be in the duration of the effort (the amount of work done) or it may be in the rate of work done. The swimmer may induce training overload either by swimming longer distances or by swimming the same distance at a faster speed. Improvement in performance comes only by increasing the demand of the conditioning effort. This is true in all five components of the conditioning program.

All experienced athletes know that the response in performance to overload is not proportional to the degree of overload. The young field hockey hopeful may run three half-hour sessions each week during preseason and improve her aerobic endurance capacity by 10 percent. Running every day or six half-hour sessions each week won't improve her aerobic capacity 20 percent; it will more likely reach only 12 to 15 percent. The body's ability to respond to overload in general and the individuality of the response to overload must always be kept in mind if frustration and discouragement with the rate of progress are to be kept in proper perspective.

Progression

The response in performance that follows the normal body response to overload is called progression. In a well-disciplined conditioning program, the normal response to overload will be reached in four to six weeks. Increasing overload in the specific areas demanded of a given sport will, in some individuals, elicit further response. But this latter response comes from progressively greater overloads extended over very prolonged periods of time. A swimmer may work for years to take a few seconds or less off his championship time. It may take endless hours of training to add another inch to the elite performance of a high jumper. Rapid responses to overload in early conditioning are followed by slow, tedious responses to the ever-increasing demands of progression.

Specificity

Each specific type of training activity must be recognized as producing a very specific conditioning response. Thus, even in early preseason conditioning, activities will usually be designed to closely simulate the movements and activities involved in the competitive sport. Aerobic endurance conditioning will occupy a more prominent part of the conditioning program of the distance runner and basketball player than that of the football candidate or the gymnast. Muscle masses involved in specific sports will receive prime attention in strength conditioning. The closer to the competing season, the more sport-specific the conditioning program will become. The hockey player will look for increasing opportunities to practice on the ice, the basketball player will dribble up and down the court, and the cross-country skier will work more and more on ski trails. The muscles themselves and the nature of the work they are going to be asked to perform are all very specific to an individual's sport.

Choosing the Right Conditioning Program

The conditioning program outlined here and its five components can meet the conditioning needs of the individual who wishes only to increase feelings of well-being, to support good health, and to enjoy taking part in various recreational activities as they become available. In addition, if pursued with greater intensity over time, this conditioning program will be very adequate to prepare a young athlete for a season of intensely competitive sport. This individual must be involved in the conditioning program for approximately an hour or more each day four or five days a week if he or she is to experience the overload and progression needed for serious sports participation. Such individuals include the high school athlete, the older adolescent involved in community-based youth sport programs, or the collegiate athlete.

What about conditioning for the millions of other youth sport participants: the preadolescent, or elementary, and junior high school–aged athletes? What is an adequate conditioning program for these athletes if they are to truly enjoy sports and be comfortably competitive with their peers?

The answer to these questions is perhaps quite obvious from the information you may have gathered from early chapters of this book. First, you should reflect on the appropriate goals of sport participation for this age group of preadolescents — those athletes under thirteen or fourteen years of age. Second, as was discussed in the chapter on the athlete's body and its behavior in response to athletic performance, there are limits to just what capabilities the preadolescent body has to respond to a conditioning program.

We believe that the appropriate goals of sports participation prior to the onset of adolescent growth and development are to have fun, encounter a variety of rewarding social experiences, learn some skills and techniques in a low-key emotional environment, and have the benefit of a generous amount of fitness-inducing physical exercise. We do not see specifically getting in shape or developing a high level of physical conditioning as an important goal for the millions of preadolescents in youth sport programs. This is especially true of the very young in their early introduction to sport. One valid reason why intense conditioning with its overload and progression of response is inappropriate at this age is that it simply cannot be looked upon as much fun. It misses the first goal of sports participation for the child.

In reviewing present-day knowledge of the preadolescent body's potential to respond to a conditioning program, we see further evidence that strongly suggests that an intense conditioning program is inappropriate. Muscles at this age in both boys and girls have little if any potential to respond with increased development of strength and endurance or increased bulk and size. The eleven-year-old girl at the tennis club shouldn't be expected to deliver an eighty-mile-an-hour serve, nor should she have as a conditioning goal ninety or 100 sit-ups and push-ups and regular visits to the weight room. She won't respond with much improvement in performance and she will be the first to know it.

Any weight-training efforts prior to the body-chemistry changes of early adolescence can be justified only as fun. The potential for developing aerobic endurance through cardiopulmonary conditioning practices is limited in the preadolescent but gradually increases with maturity.

Good conditioning and warmup involve skills and techniques just as other parts of sport performance do. When the young athlete begins organized team or club play, he or she can be expected to be introduced to the various skills and techniques of sports. It is hoped that for the preadolescent, the introduction will be by a qualified teacher who is low-keyed and pleasant.

The interested and motivated young person may begin to train with the no-equipment weight-training program outlined in this chapter and should be introduced to good stretching techniques as part of the warmup procedure for practices and games. Here again, learning the techniques of proper stretching for maintenance of flexibility for future, more serious sport participation is the goal. The approach should be relaxed, with little concern if a few repetitions are missed in the workout.

There is no doubt that good preseason, in-season, and off-season conditioning programs are of tremendous help to the committed high school athlete, the young person who, among other reasons, is into the athletic program to see just what kind of a new body he or she can develop. More often than not, the high school man or woman is highly motivated to take part in a good conditioning program. Some want to do it alone and on their own, whereas others truly enjoy various group conditioning activities. Weight-training classes, clubs, and conditioning groups are increasingly popular. Many coaches plan specific off-season team conditioning programs for their athletes. If well supervised and directed toward proper goals, conditioning activities should be encouraged among high school youths. For many it may be the beginning of a serious commitment to lifelong fitness that prepares them for enjoyable participation in a variety of active recreational-sport activities.

Attending to the five components of a conditioning program can provide an effective foundation for conditioning for high school sports as well as for fitness in later life.

Conditioning programs are appropriate only where they are compatible with proper sport goals for the age of the athlete. An age group of particular concern is the early adolescent, the individual just beginning his or her rapid gain in height and very anxious about their new and changing physique. These young people, particularly the males, often direct great effort to very intense conditioning. Intense weight training may be undertaken to increase muscle size or strength, but early adolescents may have little or no potential yet, except for a very significant increase in the risk of injury if the weight program is unsupervised and overdone. We find in this group many distance runners who run to an extreme, which, when excessive, will lead to weight loss, growth arrest, and weakness. Such excessive endurance training will make little if any contribution to physical development and athletic potential.

Early adolescents need to be informed of their developmental status. This may be best done by an understanding physician, who may give some insight as to when body changes will be such that bodies can be expected to respond to an intense conditioning program. Most vulnerable in such abuses of training are late maturers. Intense conditioning activities do not hasten the maturation process, unfortunately, and conditioning excesses by these young men should be tempered for a few years. Currently, endocrine specialists are able to provide help to some very late maturing males who become seriously distressed about their maturation and development during their junior high school and high school years. In carefully selected individuals, it is possible to hasten maturation with well-controlled endocrine therapy.

As increasing millions of Americans begin to assume an increasing level of responsibility for their own health and fitness, conditioning programs and new fitness techniques become increasingly more important and popular. The very young preadolescent will profit from being introduced to proper techniques of conditioning and warmup. The later adolescent and the high school athlete cannot fully enjoy their sports or be competitive without good conditioning programs. At this important time, as young people develop to their adult years, good physical-conditioning techniques and practices can have lifelong benefits.

6

Nutrition

Fueling the Competitive Machine

Few things regularly raise more questions in the minds of parents of young athletes than concerns about how and what they should eat. As Mom wonders whether or not the children are really getting a balanced diet, Dad knows that if Carla or Brian would only eat better, she or he surely would play better. The professional nutritionist says that all the athlete needs is a generous balanced diet; the media tell about the professional tennis star who takes hundreds of food-supplement pills each day before an important match. Whom do you listen to? How does one optimally satisfy the nutrition needs of active young competitors? Nothing less than optimal nutrition will be acceptable to the highly competitive athlete who knows that his or her diet does indeed have something important to do with performance in sport.

Unique Nutrition Needs of the Young Athlete

Active, energy-expending sport participation creates two and only two unique nutrition requirements: a need for increased food-energy intake to meet the needs of training and competition, and an increased demand for water intake to replace the sweat lost during exercise.

Satisfying these needs is essential for good performance and for the health and safety of the athlete. In addition, the young preadolescent and the older adolescent athlete have important growth needs that must be met. Long before children became involved in organized sports, childhood and adolescence were life periods when special attention was given to meeting some well-defined goals of good nutrition.

Through the eating process, humans satisfy four needs—needs that are especially important for the growing young and that take on additional importance for the physically active young participant in competitive sport. These are

- To provide energy.
- To supply chemical building blocks for growth and repair of body tissues.
- To supply essential chemicals needed for a host of body functions.

● To satisfy important psychosocial needs through interaction with family and friends during mealtime.

Living in a food-excess society, the vast majority of American young people have food available in abundance to satisfy the first three needs. National nutrition surveys find little evidence of any lack of specific nutrients in the diets of most Americans. Between 85 and 90 percent of the citizens of the United States have access to enough food to satisfy their energy needs and the nutritional needs for normal growth. The other 10 to 15 percent of citizens, who live in poverty, do not have access to adequate diets—a problem of continuing concern to many citizens' groups and political organizations.

The fourth need, to satisfy the social and behavioral requirements that humans have traditionally met through the eating process, is of increasing concern. Loss of mealtime patterns in most homes, the changing family composition, and changing life styles all raise questions as to whether young people, even in our food-abundant environment, are getting an adequate diet and the security, education, and learning experiences that come from mealtime contact with family and friends.

An axiom has evolved at the junior high school, high school, and college levels that characterizes the nutrition concerns we have for many young athletes: "The quality of the diet is directly proportionate to the quality of the environment in which it is eaten."

For almost all Americans, eating in a pleasant place with amiable people essentially guarantees that the nutritional quality of their diet will be very high and more than adequate. (One would like to always believe that the most pleasant place and most amiable people would be at the family table.) Eating alone or on the run is the surest way to eat badly. Unfortunately, too many young athletes and families eat this way.

The Young Athlete's Diet

Parents are keenly aware that the elementary school–aged child has to eat right to grow right, but a new dimension of food need has been introduced into the parenting concerns of many families: how to feed a growing young boy or girl who is now an athlete. In previous chapters the goals of good sport participation for the participant have been clearly spelled out — having fun, getting some exercise, learning some skills, and becoming familiar with some sports. These goals are in no way in conflict with the goals of good nutrition for young athletes. The goals of a positive youth-sport experience actually demand that no greater attention than usual be given to nutritional concerns that parents may perceive as important to their child's participation in sport. Actually, attempting to exploit new sport interests of young boys and girls to get them to eat more or differently can jeopardize the most important goal of youth sport participation — to have fun. The ten-year-old athlete shouldn't be cajoled into eating three health-promoting meals a day simply to make him a better quarterback, second baseman, or figure skater. He or she should have an opportunity to eat those three health-promoting and pleasant meals to make him or her a better ten-year-old. Sport interests should not be used as a weapon at mealtime. It is the parents' responsibility to provide a desirable selection of menu items at mealtime. This will determine *what* the young athlete will eat. Nature will direct the young athlete as to *how much* to eat.

Youth sport participation by the preadolescent should not be such an intense experience that satisfying excessive energy expenditures is a concern. However, monitoring water needs during practice and competition is becoming an increasing problem as very young athletes become more active in intensely competitive situations where temperature and humidity are high. The specific needs and hazards of fluid replacement in athletes will be considered later in this chapter. It is a common problem in the more intense activities of older athletes, but there is now a very real need to be alert to the fluid requirements of the elementary school–aged athlete as well.

How Sports Can Interfere with Good Nutrition

Can youth sport participation interfere with the good nutrition and good growth that result from healthy eating during childhood? "With a girl in gymnastics and two boys in soccer and baseball," said one parent, "mealtime eating together is a matter of historical interest in our family."

We sincerely believe that a good sport experience is almost essential for growing up healthy in today's society. Yet we recognize that there are other needs, priorities, and growth-promoting requirements of a happy healthy childhood. Yes, there is life beyond sports! Before family life and mealtime disappear from your household, we suggest that you hold a family council with the children, define the goals of youth sport, and then preserve a generous number of those valuable weekends, mealtimes, and other times for being together as a family.

It is equally important to be alert to the impact of more intense, competitive sport participation on the dietary needs of the adolescent athlete during his or her high school and early college years.

Scott was sent to a sports medicine clinic because of his rather rapidly deteriorating performance in training with his high school swim team. It was early in the preseason, and already Scott looked as if he was "stale." He had no specific complaints that suggested he might be ill, but he did state that he had lost between eleven and thirteen pounds during the first two months of training in the fall quarter. He was having trouble sleeping, was waking up in a profuse sweat at three or four o'clock in the morning, and was usually unable to get back to sleep. His grades in school were great — straight A's — but he was getting worried about his swim performance.

Scott also said that he was a good swimmer — state high school champion last year and ranked nationally this year — and that he had decided to take this year to find out just how good he could be. He was swimming 20,000 meters a day (about twelve miles), doing his academic work, and volunteering two evenings a week as a clerk in a storefront health clinic. He "usually" ate lunch, seldom ate breakfast, and "got dinner somewhere" every evening. Although a very intelligent young man, Scott couldn't (or wouldn't) understand why he was losing weight and underperforming in his swim workouts. The fact was that his food-energy intake was simply inadequate to meet the very generous energy expenditures of his active life style and extremely demanding training schedule.

Food-energy intake insufficient to satisfy the demands of growth, training, and daily school activities is the most common nutrition-related problem encountered among young athletes.

Like Scott, certain athletes may be overcommitted to an extent that their life styles allow no time for eating. Others come from disorganized families in which food is not regularly available or from impoverished homes in which there is no adequate food supply in the home. Whatever the reason might be, when energy intake is inadequate to meet the needs of the active young male or female athlete, there will be involuntary weight loss. Inevitably the athlete will experience a deterioration in performance. Recorded weighing once or twice each week will identify the athlete whose diet is inadequate to meet energy needs. Monitoring body weight and maintaining a desirable competing weight throughout the season are essentials for all serious competitors.

Two groups of athletes most likely to experience involuntary weight loss and poor training performance are swimmers and basketball players. These high-energy-expending individuals may find that three meals a day plus a generous evening snack are not enough to satisfy their energy needs. If a larger diet does not stabilize competing weight during the season and if adding extra meals or snacks is unacceptable to the athlete in question, the use of a convenient liquid food can be helpful by providing 500 to 1,000 kilocalories of additional food energy each day. These include products such as Ensure® and Sustacal®, available in pharmacies. This is one of the very few legitimate uses of a food supplement in sports. Taking in sufficient total food energy is essential in meeting the optimal nutrition needs of even the most sophisticated athlete.

In meeting the energy needs of the active young athlete, one should pay attention to the appropriate distribution of energy intake throughout the day. It is not uncommon to encounter athletes underperforming in afternoon practice sessions after having eaten no breakfast and only a catch-as-catch-can lunch from the campus or high school corridor vending machine. The lack of ability of these athletes to perform between three and five o'clock in the afternoon should come as no surprise. The body has very limited ability to store its most readily available energy in the form of carbohydrates before it is converted to body fat. Body fat is a good source of energy, but it must be mobilized from fat deposits and transferred to muscle cells before it can serve as an energy source for muscle work. Individuals who perform vigorous physical work during the day have always found regular food-energy intake spaced at intervals to be essential to good performance.

Eating the Right Foods

A varied diet sufficient in amount to satisfy energy needs will provide all of the essential nutrients the young athlete needs. Young athletes, their coaches, and particularly their parents are continually questioning the adequacy of the athlete's diet in providing all of those nutrients that are known to be essential for good health and athletic performance. Actually, there are approximately sixty substances recognized as so-called essential nutrients—substances that must be included in the daily diet. New dietary customs, fast foods, meatless diets, skipped meals, all raise questions as to whether the young woman or young man active in sports is adequately satisfying nutritional needs. Can you really "do your thing" with a hamburger, fries, and a shake on Friday night, a pizza on Saturday, and another fast-food dinner another night during the week? Thirty-five percent of a population of high school varsity basketball players ate their evening meal alone the night before they were interviewed for a recent nutrition study. As we've noted before, eating alone is likely to mean that you will not eat well.

Another factor that causes parents and coaches concern is the controversy surrounding special diets and dietary supplements. Some self-styled nutrition experts claim that without a particular "miracle" diet and/or supplement, we all run the risk of being chronically undernourished. Others promote the healing or empowering properties of certain herbs, remedies, or vitamins. It is difficult for the average adult—or adolescent—to verify or even sort out those claims. For the athlete such nutritional solutions are, in fact, not only useless and expensive but perhaps dangerous. It is best to consult a physician or a legitimate nutritional scientist if there is real concern about nutrition needs.

How the athlete insures the adequacy of his or her diet is important and can be the best protection against needless and expensive nutrient supplements. A simple and effective system of diet evaluation can be implemented by any parent or junior or senior high school athlete. Simply write down all of the food items eaten each day for three or four typical days. Then see if there are included in that diet appropriate representations of the four food groups that, most of us have learned, are essential to good diets.

Each day, are there two servings of dairy foods, such as milk, cheese, ice cream, or yogurt? Are there two servings of high-protein foods, such as meats, fish, poultry, legumes, or beans? Are there four servings of fruits or vegetables? Are there four servings of grain foods, such as cereals, bread, or rolls? When these twelve servings are included in each day's diet, the athlete and parent can be confident that the intake of all the known essential nutrients is adequate to meet the needs of the most intensely training athlete. This diet makes any vitamin, mineral, protein, or other food supplement unnecessary.

Recently two high school athletes were seen in their physician's office on successive days with very similar complaints. Both were feeling unwell, with marked bone pain and severe pounding headaches that had kept them awake at night and prevented them from attending classes. This unusual combination of symptoms alerted the physician to ask whether the students had been taking any vitamin pills or supplements. Indeed they had been. Both were candidates for the football team in the upcoming autumn and were trying to "bulk up" to increase their weight and potential for making the team. They were each taking three cans daily of a liquid vitamin-and-protein mixture that was being sold by the coach. Laboratory tests demonstrated that they were both suffering from vitamin A poisoning, a serious, painful intoxication that takes many weeks to get over. Later we will outline safe and effective ways to increase playing weight for improved performance in certain sports. These do not include taking expensive and potentially dangerous protein-and-vitamin supplements unless prescribed by a physician.

The athlete's diet that contains twelve servings with appropriate representation from the four food groups makes supplements unnecessary but won't meet the energy needs of the athlete. This basic four-food-group diet must be supplemented with second servings and preference foods to meet what may be very generous energy requirements. A good rule to follow is to eat first what you need (the twelve servings from the four food groups), then eat what you want to satisfy energy demands. A second rule is that if and when your diet is so inadequate that you need a vitamin or protein supplement, then you don't need a supplement, you need a better diet. The athlete can never compete on a diet of pills and powders.

Meeting the Athlete's Need
for Water and Salt

In addition to the athlete's unique need for increased intake of food energy to meet the demands of training and competing, another specific need of the athlete is replacement of the water lost in sweating. A large young athlete can lose ten or more pounds of water during an intense practice session. Basketball players in an air-conditioned gym were recently found to be losing four to six pounds of body water during a typical high school practice. Replacing these losses is critical to continued good performance and to avoiding heat disorders, such as cramps, heat exhaustion, and heat stroke. Body water is involved in several functions critical to the performance of the athlete. The body's chemical processes that provide the energy for muscle work go on in water. All of the transport functions of oxygen, nutrients, and body wastes are carried on in body water. Of most importance to the exercising athlete is the fact that the large amount of heat generated by exercising muscles is transported by water in the blood to the skin, where water is essential for the production of sweat. Body heat is dissipated most efficiently through the evaporation of sweat on exposed skin surfaces. An abundant supply of body water, first to transport muscle-generated heat and then to produce the sweat needed for evaporative cooling, is the best insurance against the complications of heat cramps, heat exhaustion, and life-threatening heat stroke.

Research in recent years has demonstrated that during exercise, losses of body water that amount to as little as 2 percent of total body weight (three pounds for a 150-pound athlete, for example) will cause a very perceptible decrease in performance. With such water loss, energy production is compromised and endurance is limited. Preventing excessive body-water deficits by fluid intake prior to exercise and at intervals during exercise can contribute measurably to performance.

Early one September Monday morning, the telephone rang. On the line were a father, a mother, and a sixteen-year-old daughter, each on his or her own extension. The daughter was a nationally ranked junior tennis champion who had just been defeated in the Midwest tennis championships played in St. Louis the preceding weekend. She had previously repeatedly defeated the person she lost the championship to, but on this particular Sunday she faded badly as the match progressed.

In the eyes of everyone, this had been a most disappointing performance. In the opinion of her father, the tennis player had not eaten right, and he had decided that she should be "talked to" about her diet. Mother wondered if she should be taking more vitamins. Neither concern would appear to have caused her to blow a particular tennis match. You don't get to the Midwest championship finals if you are suffering from malnutrition.

We asked the daughter to run upstairs and weigh herself. She came back to report that some sixteen hours after her disastrous match, she weighed eight or nine pounds less than her normal pretournament weight. Playing in the heat of a St. Louis September weekend, she had not monitored her needs for water, had lost more than ten pounds of body water, became dehydrated, and underperformed. She admitted to a rather severe, throbbing headache for several hours after the match, an early symptom of impending heat exhaustion.

Biochemists and exercise scientists have studied the nature of sweat and have come up with some very interesting and important findings for the athlete. Sweat is a very dilute body fluid when compared to other body fluids. It contains less than one third the concentration of salts that blood plasma contains, for example. It is interesting that the better conditioned the athlete, the more dilute and watery the sweat. When athletes sweat, they lose much more water than salt, when compared to other body fluids. Sweating actually results in an increase in the concentration of the body's salts and minerals. This resulting increased concentration of salts in body fluids contributes to some of the adverse consequences of sweat-water losses.

Other interesting things that have been learned about sweat is that women have fewer sweat glands and produce less sweat than men. They have greater skin surface area for every pound of body weight, however, and unlike men, they dissipate more of the heat generated in exercise by convection and conduction from the skin than by evaporation. In contrast to what was thought some years ago, women tolerate exercise in the heat as well as men.

Prior to the onset of adolescence, children do not produce sweat efficiently. They have a limited capacity for evaporative heat loss from their bodies during exercise. Recent investigations in Israel, where young children often play in very hot environments, have shown that they make a very early psychological adjustment to exertion in the heat, not noticing it as much as older individuals, even though their bodies' mechanisms for dissipating heat are poorly developed. This would put them at increased risk to heat exhaustion. Preventing heat disorders in very young athletes is an increasing concern as large numbers of preadolescent sports participants find themselves exercising in competitive situations in the heat of summer and early autumn. These very young athletes must have their practices and competitions rescheduled and modified during hot weather and have their fluid needs and the intensity of play carefully monitored. These most amateur of participants will be the last to know when they are at risk to heat exhaustion or even heat stroke. The preadolescent child is relatively new to the world of team competition and training. The risks of heat disorders in what can be an intense, highly organized athletic experience in a hot or humid environment must be new but important concerns to this age group of athletes, their coaches, and parents.

Water is the ideal beverage for replacing the fluid losses of the sweating athlete. The water should be refrigerator temperature, copious in amount, and provided in a hygienic container. So-called athlete drinks or sport drinks present several problems for the athlete losing body water through sweat. Sport drinks contain a variety of salts that when added to the body only increase the already elevated salt concentration of the dehydrated athlete. The concentration of salts and the masking sugar flavor cause these beverages to leave the stomach slowly, producing a sense of fullness and satiety. This actually discourages the athlete from taking in much-needed water. In addition, in the intense emotional environment of competition, all senses become more sensitive, making the distinctive flavor of certain beverages unpleasant, and discouraging the intake of water.

With no such disadvantages, water remains a wonderfully inexpensive, ideal beverage for replacing the water losses of sweat. Every old sailor knows that you don't maintain hydration by drinking saltwater, but American merchandisers have sold it in colorful bottles to millions of athletes.

Athletes can very effectively monitor their needs for water replacement by recognizing that any weight that is lost in a period of a few hours or even a few days is essentially all water weight.

With a pound of fat the equivalent of 3,500 kilocalories of energy, and the energy expenditure to run one mile approximately one hundred calories, it is apparent that any sudden changes in weight are not due to a significant change in the body's fat content. Nude weighing before and after each game or tournament match and drinking sufficient water to maintain a stable pretournament weight are highly desirable practices. During daily or two-a-day practices of any sport in warm, humid weather, it is recommended that all athletes record a nude weight before and after each practice. This is the surest way to be certain that fluid losses are replaced between practice sessions.

Tasting the salt in the perspiration running off the fevered brow during exercise obviously generates some real concern on the part of the athlete as to how these salt losses are to be replaced. Thus, many athletes are impressed with the much-promoted salt- and electrolyte-containing sport drinks. Fortunately there has been some very elaborate research on this at outstanding exercise-physiology laboratories, such as Ball State University labs, and in the United States Department of Agriculture's Trace Metal Research Laboratory. These recent investigations document that all of the salt and mineral losses of the most profusely sweating athlete are abundantly replaced by the elements in the generous mixed diet of the exercising athlete. The kidneys sort out what of this dietary intake is needed for replacement of sweat losses and what can be excreted as waste into the urine. Taking extra minerals in drinks or salt tablets only taxes the body's normal mechanisms for maintaining a healthy mineral balance. Particularly threatening is the use of salt tablets, which athletes often take indiscriminately. A recent football heat-stroke victim was found to have fourteen salt tablets in his stomach on X-ray examination — salt that only accentuated the consequences of his severe dehydration.

Young athletes should drink lots of clean, cool water. Eight to ten ounces drunk immediately before practice or a training run delays the adverse effects of copious sweat loss. In hot weather, coaches should schedule water breaks every twenty-five minutes and make generous amounts of water readily available to the athletes. Distance runners should drink water at each water stop during a race, and water intake should be scheduled by trainers or coaches during day-long meets, such as track events, gymnastic competitions, and wrestling tournaments. If the weather is warm and the competition particularly demanding, repeated nude weighing can give further assurance that the risks and handicaps of dehydration are being avoided.

Eating Before and During Competition

The annals of sport are replete with stories about pregame eating experiences that turned certain defeat into glorious victory. Soon after joining the sports medicine clinic at the University of Washington, one of us was asked by a young track star, "Say, Doc, why is pizza such a fast food?" The response he got—complete ignorance of why pizza is a "fast" food, or even that it had ever been known to make people run fast—cost medical science some credibility in the eyes of this speedy quarter-miler. In the not-too-distant past, some local runner had enjoyed a large intake of pizza and ran the best race of his career. Others merely put two and two together, and to the satisfaction of the pizza-parlor operator and a few subsequent generations of runners at this school, pizza became a fast food. The pizza was traditionally eaten at one particular establishment (not the best in the area), on Fridays before every Saturday track meet and was actually eaten by all of the believers in complete silence!

The psychological impact of the pregame meal should not be minimized or ignored. It can serve the needs of the athlete and the team to exploit the very real emotional impact of food and eating together. In planning the pregame meal, you should keep in mind the most important thing: that it should be planned. A well-planned eating experience tells athletes that they are being well prepared to handle their responsibilities in the upcoming competition.

Here are guidelines for planning the pregame meal for an athlete or a team:

- Locate a suitable place where the team or athletes can be together and can concentrate on the upcoming competition.
- Include in the menu any food that the athletes "know" will make them win.
- The meal is best if it is low in fat, modest in protein, and high in carbohydrate.
- The meal should be modest in amount.

- The menu should avoid those foods that carry a greater-than-usual risk of food poisoning, such as cream gravies, turkey, and cream pastries.

- Fatty foods leave the stomach slowly and thus should be eaten five or more hours before a game.

Having had nothing to eat for several hours, many athletes will play "hungry." Coaches and athletes should all learn the old rule, Saturday's game is played on Wednesday, Thursday, and Friday's food intake. The pregame meal is not the time to try to provide all of the energy for some high-energy-expending competition. A very simple pregame menu that can be arranged in any commercial eating establishment, is not expensive, and can be eaten two and a half to three hours before the game includes the following:

- Lean beef or chicken sandwiches

- Pitchers of fruit punch or fruit juice

- A large Jell-O salad

- Generous servings of sherbert and cake or cookies

A big steak dinner is a fine postgame meal for the affluent team, either to celebrate or to forget and get ready for the next game. It is a poor choice as a pregame meal.

As young athletes become increasingly serious about their sports commitments, there are those who direct their precompetition anxieties to their stomachs and upper gastrointestinal tracts. They tend to be pregame vomiters. These delightfully intense individuals can profit by being introduced to pregame complete liquid meals. To date those liquid meals suitable for the athlete have been hospital products designed to meet all of the nutritional needs of people who must subsist on liquid diets. The products are of high pharmaceutical quality and are very well tolerated. They come in small cans, which can be chilled and sipped up to an hour or two before game time. Certain athletes find these products the answer to food intake during day-long competition, such as track meets, gymnastic competitions, and wrestling tournaments. Ensure® and Sustacal® are examples of products that are available in most hospital pharmacies.

Special attention should be given to the food needs of the team of young athletes away from home, those who are spending an evening in a motel between episodes of competition. These young people are at considerable risk for gastronomical disasters and compromised performance the following day. It is as important to plan evening eating as it is to plan all mealtime food intake. Sherbert and cookies make a good high-carbohydrate evening snack. By providing such refreshments, the coach or manager may keep the athletes away from vending machines and fast-food establishments and make a positive contribution to the energy taken into the next day's game.

Special Nutritional Needs of the High School Athlete

As young men and women begin to make their serious commitment to sport during their high school years, they encounter nutrition and training procedures designed specifically to optimize their potential for performance in a given sport. At the high school level, the most common procedures are cutting weight for participation in strength or weight-matched sports, building up (increasing body weight), and loading up on glycogen for endurance sports. All these practices can be safe when properly carried out and can contribute to the participant's success and enjoyment in the sport. The supervision of the team physician, family physician, or professional nutritionist may be called upon in initiating these special nutrition practices in the young, growing athlete.

Weight Control in Sports

Many late-maturing, small individuals are attracted to interscholastic wrestling because the competitors in this sport are matched on a weight basis and the small size of the individual is not a handicap. In addition to small late maturers in the lower weight classes, many young men weighing 120 to 150 pounds who are too small to be competitive in football or basketball find wrestling an attractive winter sport. In fact, there is a disproportionate number of participants in the weight classes between 120 and 145 pounds, so competition for varsity positions may become very intense. The competitors often try to manipulate their weights to compete in a weight class in which they have the best chance of being on the first team. This can lead to serious abuses, such as fluid restriction, starvation, and use of diuretic pills and cathartics. Coaches and wrestling candidates should know that the most effective goal for competition in a weight-matched sport is to take into competition the maximum amount of strength, endurance, and quickness for every pound of body weight. In other words, the athlete should go into competition with a minimum level of fatness compatible with optimal fitness. The estimated minimal-fatness level of 5 to 7 percent of body weight satisfies this goal and has been found to be the level of fatness of high-performing wrestlers and other elite athletes in weight-matched sports. It is recommended that every candidate for the wrestling team have his body fat estimated six to eight weeks before the competing season begins. When the athlete knows what his fatness level is, he can calculate what his competing weight would be at 5 to 7 percent body fat. He then knows that he can be most competitive at that weight, allowing three to four pounds for growth during the season. Most candidates have excess fat that must be lost to reach their desired competing weights. This can be done by increasing their energy expenditures with after-school, preseason conditioning and by limiting their diets to no less than 2,000 calories each day. The rate of fatness loss should be no greater than two or three pounds per week. Thus it is essential to initiate the program well before the competing season. There is no way in which fat can be reduced rapidly without sacrificing normal growth and reducing muscle.

Wrestling programs should also be encouraged to increase the number of positions for competitors in classes that attract the largest numbers of candidates—the 120- to 145-pound weight classes.

In certain strength-related sports, such as men's gymnastics and figure skating, fat in excess of the minimum compatible with optimal fitness will hinder performance. As in wrestling, estimating fatness and reducing it with modest diet reductions and increased energy expenditure at a carefully controlled rate will be compatible with good performance and good health.

"Bulking Up" for Sport

Each year hundreds of thousands of young adolescents try to increase their body weight and size to increase their potential for sport performance. Football-team aspirants are a significant percentage of these youths. In a study of forty-eight varsity football players in four different high schools, more than two thirds of them had used special diets, drugs, and supplements to try to increase body weight at some time during their high school careers. The young person trying to increase body size for a sport needs professional supervision by a physician who appreciates the sincere commitment of the athlete and the importance of his or her concern with body size.

An interested physician can play a critical role in a young person's weight-gaining efforts by estimating maturity status and growth potential and recommending safe and effective methods for weight gain. The athlete must realize that only an increase in muscle mass will increase his or her potential as an athlete. Simply getting fatter will accomplish nothing and may threaten later health. The athlete must also know that only muscle work will increase muscle size and muscle mass. There is no hormone, vitamin, protein, or nutritional supplement that will increase muscle tissue. The athlete trying to gain weight must follow a professionally supervised weight-training program of muscle work and must ingest the increased amount of food needed to support the increased growth of new muscle. This more caloric diet should be one low in cholesterol and saturated fats, limited in salt, and high in fiber content. (The American Heart Association has an excellent diet of this type.) A diet for weight-gaining purposes in high school can be a very positive nutrition-education experience for young athletes and their families. In our experience a conscientious high school athlete can gain as much as one to one and one-half pounds a week with a well-supervised program and a high degree of enthusiastic compliance.

Glycogen Loading for the Endurance Athlete

Relatively few young athletes at the junior or senior high school level become involved in competitions that are positively influenced by so-called glycogen loading, or supercompensation. Long-distance cross-country skiing and marathon running are classic examples of sports in which maximizing the concentration of muscle starch — glycogen — enhances the athlete's performance. Muscle glycogen concentrations are maximized by vigorously exercising the muscles used in the sport event for three or four days while maintaining a controlled amount of carbohydrate in the diet. The resulting depletion of glycogen in the muscle stimulates muscle enzymes to overcompensate the level of glycogen that is retained in the muscle when the athlete then takes in a high-carbohydrate diet. While ingesting the high-carbohydrate diet, the athlete must reduce the intensity of the training for four days prior to the competition. Glycogen loading is a very demanding regime and appropriate for seriously committed athletes in true endurance events.

7

Sport Injuries

When the Colors of Sports Are Black and Blue

Fortunately, serious injuries are not common in sports. This is particularly true for athletes less than fourteen years of age. Their small size and limited strength and aggressiveness combine with safety rules and adult supervision to help minimize the risk of significant injury. Sport injuries become more common in high school, where the intensity of competition increases along with the size and strength of the participants. These older and stronger athletes are more capable of causing injury to themselves and to their opponents.

Happily, regardless of age, most athletes will not suffer serious sport injuries, and when properly managed, injuries will limit training and competition for no more than a few days. Because responsibility for the recognition and management of sport-related injuries often falls on parents, there is some essential information that you should have about their nature and treatment.

What Is a Sport Injury?

The sore muscles Dad suffered the morning after a three-hour volleyball game at last summer's office picnic is not technically a sport injury. Those hurts are merely Nature's way of telling Dad that he should probably do some regular physical exercise. There are certain symptoms, however, that indicate a true sport injury and should be recognized as such by the athlete, the coach, and the parent. These include

- Bleeding
- Mental confusion or loss of consciousness
- Numbness or tingling of an extremity
- A recognizable deformity of any body part
- Instability of any joint, such as a knee that "wobbles"
- The sound of tearing or ripping at the time of injury
- Localized swelling or pain
- Absence of a full range of motion of any joint

An individual with any of these symptoms should not return to play or practice until a very specific diagnosis of the nature of the injury has been made and the symptoms of injury have completely disappeared. Any of these injuries can easily be made worse by continued participation. Unable to move normally and protect themselves when injured, athletes with any of these symptoms are at high risk to a new injury.

The most common sport-related injuries are the so-called overuse injuries, the too-much, too-soon, too-fast injuries. These injuries result from the improper or excessive use of some body part, most often tendons and muscles. Overuse injuries are often identified with certain sports or types of activities. There is the jogger's heel, the jumper's knee, the tennis elbow, the swimmer's shoulder, the Little League elbow, and so on. All are the result of overuse of a specified muscle or tendon unit in training for a certain sport.

In collision sports, such as football, wrestling, ice hockey, and lacrosse, the most common injuries are bumps, bruises, and lacerations. In both collision and running sports, muscles, tendons, and ligaments can be stretched or torn in strains and sprains, although most of these possible injuries tend to be minor ones.

The injured athlete or the parents of the youth sport participant must assume primary responsibility for the proper management of a sport injury, initiating and following a safe and effective management plan that will assure the athlete's return to participation as quickly and as safely as possible. Prompt treatment and effective follow-through on a sound treatment plan are most important. Postponing care or failing to follow the prescribed treatment plan will prolong discomfort, hamper performance, and greatly increase the risk of reinjury.

Athletes should be told to inform their coach or trainer about any injury immediately so that they can be promptly treated and returned to the game or practice as soon as possible. Attempting to tough it out and play through pain can harm both the athlete and the team. It is better to stay out of practice for two or three days while an injury is being properly treated and return to action only when fully recovered.

Things Not to Do If Injured in Sport

Here are some important don'ts to emphasize to your young athlete:

- **Don't** try to hide an injury. Report the injury to the coach or trainer.

- **Don't** apply treatment other than simple first aid until a specific diagnosis has been made by the trainer or a doctor.

- **Don't** apply heat to an injury without orders from the doctor. A widely held but mistaken belief is that heat helps a new injury. As we'll see, it can actually make things worse rather than better.

- **Don't** use an injured part if it hurts. More hurting means more injury.

- **Don't** take any drugs unless they are prescribed by a physician.

- **Don't** tape or splint an injured part without specific instructions from a doctor.

- **Don't** go back to practice or competition until you have a full range of motion, full strength (both sides are equally strong), and full function of the injured part.

These don'ts should be modified only under the direct orders of a physician or a certified trainer (not a volunteer or student trainer). The quickest and safest way to get back into active participation is to limit activity as long as there is any pain or swelling, then to follow rigidly the prescribed rehabilitation program, which will include a schedule of specifically planned exercises. In specialized sport medicine clinics, the patient problem most frequently seen is the athlete with an inadequately rehabilitated sport injury who returned to his sport and was reinjured. In a recent large study of high school football injuries, 50 percent of those injured were reinjured when they returned to participation — a sad commentary on injury management.

Things to Do When Injured

The athlete's first responsibility when injured is to get out of the game or practice. Continued participation may make the injury worse and may place the athlete at increased risk to another injury. A healthy substitute is better for the team than an injured all-star.

When leaving the field or court, the athlete should avoid using the injured part. The player should support an injured arm or wrist (with a sling if possible) and get support so he or she won't walk on an injured leg or ankle.

Promptly apply the only first-aid treatment that is safe for treatment of a sports injury without professional advice — ICE (*I* for ice, *C* for compression, and *E* for elevation). Never apply heat to a sports injury unless it is ordered by a physician.

The ICE treatment is easily applied and easily available on the sidelines at games and practices. All that is needed are plastic bags (from the supermarket produce counter), crushed ice (from a nearby drive-in or school cafeteria), and a picnic cooler, which holds the bags of crushed ice and some wet four-inch elastic bandages.

To apply the ICE treatment, remove any part of the uniform that surrounds the injured area and elevate the arm or leg above the level of the heart. Apply one layer of the cold, wet elastic bandage on the skin directly over the injury, put the plastic bag of ice on the bandage, and firmly wrap the remainder of the bandage around the bag of ice. Keep the ice and the compression wrap on the elevated, immobilized injury for twenty-five to thirty minutes. As long as there is pain and/or swelling, keep the injury elevated. Avoid standing or walking on a painful leg or ankle before or after the ice application. ICE treatment for twenty-five to thirty minutes may be applied four or more times a day for a few days following an injury. If pain or swelling persists, see a physician.

When a girl sprains her ankle in a basketball game and its supporting ligaments are stretched and torn, or when a wide receiver strains and ruptures the fibers of a hamstring muscle, a sequence of events occurs that is common to all such sport injuries. Blood vessels are damaged and some will break, allowing blood and fluid to accumulate in the injured area. This causes increased pressure, swelling, and pain, and the pressure and swelling cause further damage and injury to the surrounding tissues.

This reaction of the body to injury has a protective function as well. The pain of the initial injury causes the muscles of the injured area to go into further painful spasms. This limits movement and discourages the use of the injured area, thereby preventing further injury.

The ICE treatment helps in three important ways: First, applying ice chills the bruised or injured area, causing blood vessels to contract and reducing circulation to the injured area — quite the opposite of what heat applications might do. Second, applying pressure with the elastic bandage inhibits the accumulation of blood and fluids in the area, thereby minimizing painful and damaging swelling. Finally, elevating the injury decreases fluid accumulation in the injured area, puts the area at rest, and helps reduce painful muscle spasms. When applied promptly and repeatedly, ICE treatments significantly reduce the discomfort and period of limited activity resulting from an injury. Another important factor is that when properly applied, ICE treatments can do no harm to any type of injury. Almost anything else — including heat applications — can cause harm in some instances.

The story of Mark, a guard on a boy's club basketball team for thirteen- and fourteen-year-olds, is a case in point. He was playing in a city-wide postseason tournament when in the middle of the third quarter, he broke free for a lay-up. As he came down from the basket, his foot came down on the foot of a trailing opponent. He fell heavily, with his weight on the outer edge of his foot. It collapsed under him, painfully stretching and tearing portions of the ligaments on the outside of his left ankle.

The physician in attendance at the tournament examined the ankle, diagnosed a moderately severe sprain, and determined that an X-ray examination wasn't needed at the time. A volunteer trainer properly equipped with plastic ice bags and chilled, wet elastic bandages applied ice and compression to the injured ankle and had Mark elevate the ankle on an upper bleacher during the remainder of the game.

At the end of the game, supported by his teammates, Mark showered and was driven home, where thirty-minute ICE treatments were applied three more times before bedtime. A suitcase was used to elevate the foot of Mark's bed while he slept. (A pillow under the ankle is not recommended; it only stays in place for about the first three minutes of sleep.)

Mark remained at home watching the NCAA basketball championships with his father during the weekend. He used crutches rented from a local pharmacy for essential movements and applied the ICE treatment every three hours for thirty minutes. On Monday he used the crutches to go to school, applied the ICE treatment in the nurse's office during his two free periods, and checked in with his physician after school. By now there remained only slight swelling and some discoloration around the injured ankle. Mark could walk without pain. He was now allowed "essential walking" without crutches and began a series of progressive muscle-strengthening exercises.

The spring soccer season was to start in three weeks, and thus

Mark was conscientious about his rehabilitation program. By doing the ankle-strengthening exercises three times each day, he was able to begin jogging in a week, to do full running in two weeks, and to cut and do sharp turns in three weeks. Mark was able to work out with his soccer team in time. He had also learned how to wrap his ankle and was advised to do so when exercising for the next year.

Although it took nearly a month, this was an excellent recovery from a moderately severe ankle sprain—a very common injury. The rapid and complete recovery was the result of repeated use of the ICE treatment, support and crutches to avoid further injury to the area, and the program of rehabilitation exercises. Mark's future participation in sport will not be limited by a persistent weak ankle that so many athletes complain of.

Preventing Sport Injuries

Everyone involved in youth sports should constantly seek practical ways to minimize the risk of sport injury. Here are some things parents, program directors, and athletes can do to reduce the risk of injury:

- Assure that competition is between persons with similar levels of proficiency, maturity, size, and strength. This is particularly important in the collision sports, where the risk of injury is greatest. The less-skilled and smaller players get more than their share of injuries in such sports.

- Be sure that athletes are at appropriate levels of conditioning before they turn out for practice or attempt vigorous competition. A good idea for athletes is to talk to the coach two or three months prior to the first workouts and get suggestions for a preseason conditioning program. The unconditioned athlete gets injured early in the season, sometimes seriously. Basic conditioning guidelines are presented in this book in the chapter on conditioning.

- Be certain that protective equipment is available and used. Protective equipment has been developed and provided for good reasons. Be sure it fits, that it doesn't need repair, and that it is used properly.

- Most sports are played on the feet. Be certain that shoes and socks fit and that socks are clean and without holes. Many troublesome foot problems can be prevented.

- Don't wear jewelry in active sports. Neck jewelry can be dangerous; rings can produce serious finger injury by getting caught in basket nets, uniforms, and so on.

- Practice good hygiene. Skin infections are common among athletes and can keep an athlete out of training for a week or more of expensive treatment. They can also spread to other team members. Showering with an antibacterial soap daily is a good practice to reduce the risk of skin infections. Keep all uniforms laundered and clean.

- Fingernails should always be trimmed shorter than the tip of the finger to prevent painful scratches and potentially serious eye injuries. This is especially important in basketball.

- Never play with a fever. Otherwise mild, common viral infections can become serious illnesses following a hard workout or game. Stay home; the risk of passing an infection on to other team members should always be avoided. A good rule is that with fever over 100 degrees, stay home and get well.

- Whether at a school, playground, or community gymnasium, take a minute to be sure that anything a player may run into or get injured from is well away from the playing area. Bicycles, automobiles, benches, lawn mowers, sprinklers, scorers' tables, and other obstacles can all cause serious injuries.

Be Prepared for an Emergency

Most injuries occurring in sports are minor, but on very rare occasions, serious, life-threatening injuries occur. These emergencies usually have to be managed on the scene before any medical help is available. In professionally supervised school sports, at practice and during games, the coach or trainer will be responsible for a plan of action to be followed in an emergency. In the community sport programs in which most children participate or at unsupervised pickup games, there will be no professionally trained coach or trainer on hand.

In these situations we strongly recommend to volunteer coaches, parents, and athletes over the age of twelve that they do one thing before getting involved any further in sports: Get certified in CPR (cardiopulmonary resuscitation). CPR training is available through the American Red Cross, local fire departments, schools, or Boy Scout programs. Training in CPR teaches you the simple life-saving techniques that can keep a seriously injured athlete alive until emergency medical help arrives.

An accident or injury to an athlete that results in any of the following symptoms presents a serious emergency that demands the skills of CPR training and prompt medical assistance:

- Not breathing
- Unconscious
- Bleeding
- In shock — particularly during hot weather

Injured athletes in these conditions can die before medical assistance arrives on the scene if someone isn't prepared to initiate thoughtful action.

Before you as a parent attend your daughter or son's next game or practice, or before you as a young athlete start that pickup game with your friends, take ten seconds and think through exactly how you would get emergency help if one of those very rare but life-threatening injuries should occur.

You must know

- Where is there a telephone?
- Who has the coins to make it work?
- Whom do you call for help?
- What is the location of the field or gym?
- Will the emergency vehicle be able to get on the field? If there is a locked gate, who has the key?

If you don't know these things, you may be helpless when the crisis occurs. Someone's son or daughter or teammate could die because no one was prepared for the unexpected.

Earlier we listed some important don'ts for sport injuries in general. The following recommendations are even more critical because of the life-threatening nature of some serious injuries:

- **Don't** move an unconscious player any more than needed for CPR.
- **Don't** move any player who can't move all four extremities freely.
- **Don't** remove the helmet from any unconscious player. You may seriously compound a possible injury to the spine.
- **Don't** use ammonia capsules to attempt to revive the player who may be unconscious or "dinged." They can complicate a neck or spine injury and may cause face and eye burns.

Steve and his friends were to be the stalwarts of this year's local Babe Ruth baseball team. They decided to get together for an informal Saturday afternoon game the week before practice was to begin. Shortly after the game started, Steve raced for second base and slid headfirst toward the bag. As he slid, his left arm caught on the base and his legs became tangled with the feet of the second baseman, who was covering the bag. Steve's back bent in a severe arch. He heard a crack and felt an excruciating pain. As his teammates gathered around, he cried out that he couldn't move his legs. Brad, the catcher, took charge and ordered that no one move or even touch Steve. Brad ran to the bench, opened his gear bag, and took out a card and a twenty-five-cent piece he had taped inside. He ran to the telephone booth at the parking lot. Depositing the quarter, he dialed 911 and reported the following: "There has been an injury at the baseball diamond in Seahurst Park at Fifteenth and Collins streets. A player has hurt his back and can't move his legs."

In less than five minutes, medics were on the field. Steve was moved by expert medical-aid personnel and within minutes was in the hospital and being taken care of by specialists. Steve had broken a bone in his back, but his legs were not permanently paralyzed. He actually played the last four games of the season.

Lots of people say that Steve was very lucky. But Brad, Steve, Steve's parents, and his doctors know that luck had little to do with it. Someone — Brad — knew what to do and was prepared to do it. Steve was lucky all right — lucky that Brad was there, for the specialist told Steve's parents that he could easily have been paralyzed if he had been moved incorrectly.

Much of the fun and satisfaction of sport participation comes from extending oneself to maximum effort. Such stresses may on occasion result in injury. Although most injuries are not serious, they do interfere temporarily with one's ability to compete and can result in more serious injuries if not cared for properly. Know how to manage the more common, less severe injuries that will be brought home by young athletes. Don't let them become more severe than need be or lead to a needlessly prolonged period of disability. Never encourage an athlete to play with pain. And always be prepared to act effectively if the rare instance of serious injury should arise.

8

Athletic Stress

Developing Coping Skills Through Sports

Sport participation places both physical and psychological demands on athletes. From youth leagues to the professional level, athletes are forced to cope with the stresses that arise from competing head-on with others in activities that are important to the athletes and others, such as parents, coaches, and peers. Some athletes learn to cope successfully with these stresses, and for them sports are enjoyable and challenging. Others who are unable to cope find sport participation to be a stressful and threatening experience.

There is no question that people differ in their ability to cope successfully with stressful situations. Such differences result primarily from the attitudes and coping skills that are learned during the childhood and adolescent years. Athletics can be an important arena in which such skills are learned. In a sense, the athletic experience can be a sort of laboratory for trying out and mastering ways of dealing with stress.

Through their athletic experiences, youngsters can develop attitudes, beliefs, and coping skills that carry over into other areas of their lives. Childhood is the best time to learn stress-management skills, and in this chapter we are concerned with what you as a parent can do to help in this process.

What Is Stress?

Before discussing ways of reducing stress, we need to explore what we mean by stress. An examination of what stress is should give us some clues on how to cope successfully with it.

We typically use the term *stress* in two different but related ways. First, we use the term to refer to *situations* in our lives that place physical or psychological demands on us. Family conflicts, work pressures, or school problems are examples of events that might cause us to say that "there is a lot of stress in my life right now."

The second way in which we use the term is to refer to our mental, emotional, and behavioral *responses* to these demanding situations. Worry, anger, tension, or grief are examples of such reactions, as are loss of appetite, sleep difficulties, and inability to get one's mind off the problem. We are referring to such reactions when we say, "I'm feeling a lot of stress right now."

In the accompanying figure, we present an analysis of stress that takes both the situation and the person's reactions into account. As

The Nature of Stress

you can see, four major elements are involved, the first being the external situation that is making some sort of physical or psychological demand on the person. Typically we view our emotions as being directly triggered by these situations, as shown in such statements as "He makes me furious when he says that" or "The kids drove me nuts today."

But the true emotional triggers are not in the external situation; they are in our minds. Situations in and of themselves have no meaning to us until we *appraise* them, which is the second element of stress. Through the process of appraisal, we perceive and give meaning to situations. This appraisal process has several parts. We appraise the nature of the situation and the demands it is placing upon us. At the same time we appraise the resources that we have to deal with it. We judge, in other words, how capable we are of coping with the situation. We also judge the probable consequences of coping or failing to cope with the situation and the meaning of those consequences for us.

The emotional responses that we call stress are likely to occur when we view ourselves as incapable of coping with a high-demand situation that has potentially harmful consequences for us. In response to such appraisals, our body instantaneously mobilizes itself to deal with the emergency, and we experience physiological arousal, the third element of stress. This inborn fight-or-flight response involves a general arousal of the body. Heart rate increases, blood is rushed to the muscles, blood pressure and muscle tension increase, perspiration may occur, and so forth. All of us are familiar with the way our body becomes aroused when we perceive that we are threatened or in danger.

The fourth element in our analysis of stress involves the way in which the person responds to the situation. Responses may be mental, as when a quarterback tries to figure out which play to call, or they may be physical or social responses, such as shooting a free throw or dealing with an angry teammate.

To view this sequence in action, let us consider Kevin, who is at the plate with two outs, the bases loaded, and his team trailing by a run in the last inning. He is facing a pitcher who has struck him out twice without his even hitting a foul ball. He views the pitcher as being too tough for him (demands exceed resources). He thinks that if he strikes out again, his parents, coach, and teammates will be disappointed in him and he will be disappointed in himself. These appraisals of the situation, his ability to cope with it, and the negative consequences he expects combine to produce predictable physical results. His mouth is as dry as a ball of cotton. His legs are shaking and he can barely hold the bat. His stomach is churning and his heart is pounding. His responses to the situation involve trying to concentrate on the pitcher and swing only at balls that are in the strike zone. Whatever the outcome of his actions, it is clear that Kevin is experiencing a high degree of stress.

Kevin's stress response to the situation seems quite natural. Most of us would probably react in much the same way. Yet some would argue that situations such as this place too much stress on children before they are psychologically equipped to handle it. Are youth sports indeed too stressful for children?

How Stressful Are Youth Sports?

Researchers have used several approaches to try to measure the stressfulness of the youth sport setting. In several studies devices were attached to children so that their physiological arousal could be measured directly, through a method known as telemetry. Such measuring instruments send a radio signal to a receiver so that physiological responses, such as heart rate, can be measured while the subject is behaving normally. These studies have shown that children can experience high levels of arousal during athletic contests. For example, heart rates averaging nearly 170 beats per minute have been recorded in male Little League Baseball players while they were at bat or in the on-deck circle.

The problem with this approach, however, is that physiological measures by themselves cannot tell us exactly *which* emotion is being experienced by the child. In some children elevated heart rates may reflect high levels of anxiety, while in others they may reflect great anticipation and excitement about going to bat. We can't tell simply by measuring the level of arousal.

To get around this problem, another approach has been to ask children to fill out rating scales of how tense, anxious, or worried they are at a particular moment. In a series of studies conducted at UCLA, Tara Scanlan and Michael Passer obtained anxiety ratings from boys and girls immediately before and after youth soccer matches. They found that most children reported rather low levels of anxiety at both points in time. However, about 20 percent of the children reported high levels of stress before the game, and many of the children reported high anxiety after games that their teams had lost.

Thus, there is evidence that sports can be stressful, at least for some children. But we need to go one step further and ask how stressful sports are compared with other activities in which children participate. To answer this important question, Julie Simon and Rainer Martens of the University of Illinois obtained anxiety ratings from nine- to fourteen-year-old boys before a number of different activities, including various individual and team sports, school tests, and band solos. The researchers found that none of the sports they studied aroused as much anxiety as band solos. Moreover, wrestling was the only sport that was more anxiety-arousing than classroom tests in school. Of the various sports studied, individual contact sports seemed to arouse the highest levels of pre-event anxiety. But, like the UCLA researchers, Simon and Martens reported that some of the young athletes claimed extremely high levels of stress before competing, regardless of the sport.

Taken together, the research results suggest that sport participation is not exceedingly stressful for most children, especially in comparison with other activities in which children have their performance evaluated. But it is equally clear that the sport setting is capable of producing high levels of stress for certain children. Instead of finding athletic competition enjoyable and challenging, some children undoubtedly experience threats and anxiety in the competitive sport setting. Such youngsters could surely benefit from attempts to help them cope more effectively with the stress that threatens their enjoyment of the sport activity.

How Stress Affects Young Athletes

Fear and anxiety are unpleasant states that most people try to avoid. There is evidence that this is precisely what many stress-ridden young athletes do. Avoiding or dropping out of sports is one of the ways in which some children escape from an activity they find threatening rather than pleasant. Canadian researchers Terry Orlick and Cal Botterill held extensive interviews with children who were not participating in sports. Many of these had quit sports programs. A large proportion of these youngsters indicated to them that they would like to compete but were fearful of performing poorly or of failing to make a team. Stress can thus reduce enjoyment and participation in athletics.

Stress affects not only how athletes feel but also how they perform. All of us have seen athletes fall apart or "choke" under high levels of stress. When under great stress even gifted athletes can perform poorly. A key to understanding how stress affects performance is the relationship between physical arousal and performance shown in the following figure.

This relationship takes the form of an inverted U. When arousal is absent or extremely low, athletes frequently describe themselves as flat and do not perform as well as they are able. As arousal increases, so does performance, but only up to a certain point. Beyond that optimal arousal point at the top of the inverted U, arousal begins to interfere with behavior, and we get a drop-off in performance. Research has also shown that the more complicated or difficult the task, the less arousal it takes to interfere with performance. Thus, it takes less arousal to interfere with a figure skater or a golfer's performance than with a sprinter or a weight lifter's.

High-stress athletes who cannot control their emotions are likely to experience higher-than-optimal levels of arousal and to perform poorly. The failure experiences that result only serve to reinforce these athletes' fears and undermine their confidence. Thus, a vicious circle involving anxiety, impaired performance, and increased anxiety can result. Many young athletes never succeed in achieving their potential in sports because of their inability to control their anxiety.

One other effect of stress should be noted. There is mounting medical evidence that high levels of chronic stress can impair health. The physical nature of the stress response taxes the resources of the body and appears to make children and adults alike more susceptible to illness and disease. Sports medicine specialists have observed many cases of health breakdowns of various sorts among highly stressed children. Not long ago, we saw a twelve-

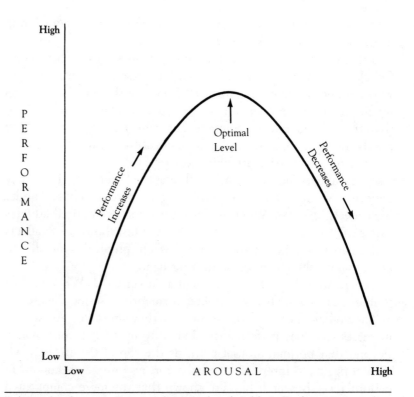

High

P
E
R
F
O
R
M
A
N
C
E

Optimal
Level

Performance
Increases

Performance
Decreases

Low

Low   AROUSAL   High

Relationship between Emotional Arousal and Athletic Performance

year-old competitive figure skater who was experiencing so much stress related to her sport that she developed an ulcer. This is surely a high and unnecessary price to pay for the pursuit of athletic excellence!

Stress affects physical well-being in yet another way: Studies of both college and high school athletes show that stressful life changes are related to an increased likelihood of injury. Sports medicine specialists have also observed that athletes who find participation to be stressful and unpleasant often appear to take longer to recover from injuries. It may be that in some cases an athlete finds in an injury a temporary and legitimate haven from the stresses of competition.

We see, then, that stress can have many effects on athletes of all ages and that most of them are negative. Thus, athletes who develop coping skills that allow them to bear up under the pressure of competition, to be mentally tough in the face of athletic challenge and adversity, have a definite advantage.

Reducing and Controlling Athletic Stress

Given the negative effects of high levels of athletic stress, what are some ways in which stress can be reduced? To answer this question, let us return to the analysis of stress shown in the previous figure. We described four elements in the stress cycle: the situation, the behavior, physical arousal, and the appraisal of the situation. Stress can be reduced at any one of these four levels.

The first way in which stress can be reduced is to change aspects of the situation that create unnecessary stress for young athletes. For example, we are all well aware that coaches and parents can create stress by their actions. Many young athletes experience unnecessary stress because adults put undue pressure on them to perform well. Coaches who are punishing and abusive to children can create a very stressful and unenjoyable environment. Similarly, parents who yell at their children during games or withdraw their love if the young athlete lets them down can create a situation in which the youngster "runs scared" much of the time. Eliminating such actions by coaches and parents can reduce unnecessary stress. Moreover, by creating an environment in which teammates support rather than criticize one another, coaches can help to reduce stress in the athletic situation.

There are several other ways to change the situation to make it less stressful. One approach is to decrease the demands of the competitive situation. Some youth leagues organize themselves so that children compete against others of their own ability, size, or weight instead of age. This increases the chances for all the children to experience success and enjoyment, and it reduces the chances of smaller and less-skilled players being injured if the sport is a contact sport.

A second approach to reducing stress lies in helping the athlete to behave more efficiently. It is quite natural to feel insecure when we don't have the skills to cope with a situation. Many young athletes experience this insecurity when they first learn a sport. As their athletic skills increase, they become better able to deal with the demands of the athletic situation, and their stress decreases. Thus, working with a child to improve skills is one way parents can reduce athletic stress.

A third point at which stress can be reduced is at the level of physical arousal. Training in the skill of relaxing their bodies has proved helpful to athletes of all ages, since it is impossible to be relaxed and tense at the same time. Later in this chapter we will outline a program that you can use to teach your young athlete this valuable skill.

The fourth and probably most fundamental approach to reducing or preventing stress is to influence how the young athlete appraises athletic situations. Appraisal is important because it involves basic attitudes, beliefs, viewpoints, and ways of interpreting reality which trigger our emotional reactions. As a parent you are a powerful influence on the way your child comes to view his or her world. The miniature world of sport provides you with opportunities to convey healthy attitudes and viewpoints to your youngster.

Preventing or Reducing Fear of Failure

Aside from fears of physical injury that produce stress for some athletes, most athletic stress arises from the fact that sport is an important social situation. The athlete's performance is visible to everyone present, and it is constantly being evaluated by the athlete and significant people in his or her life. Many athletes dread the possibility of failure and fear the disapproval of others. Many of them feel that their athletic performance is a reflection of their basic self-worth, and they therefore have a great need to avoid failing. They feel that failure will diminish them in their own eyes and in those of others.

These ideas do not arise in a vacuum. They almost always have been communicated to youngsters by their parents or other important adults. This is not surprising, because the basic beliefs underlying such ideas are very widespread and accepted in our culture. Helping your child learn a healthy philosophy of achievement and approval thus requires that basic beliefs underlying fears of failure be directly challenged and confronted.

As our analysis of stress implies, thoughts and feelings are closely interrelated. Although we are used to perceiving situations as directly causing our feelings, a moment of reflection shows clearly that this is not the case. If it were, we could not account for the fact that people often show great differences in the ways they respond emotionally to the very same situation. When one person becomes completely unglued, another remains totally calm and seemingly unaffected. When one individual becomes fearful, another becomes angry. We could not account for such differences if situations directly caused our emotions.

This is where our mental processes enter the picture. Situations have no meaning until we give them meaning by the ways in which we appraise them. In other words, it is our viewpoint about the situation that determines our emotional response. These viewpoints are often affected by deeply held beliefs that we adopt while we are growing up. Unfortunately, some of the beliefs that are very widespread in our culture do not make much sense at all when examined closely. The problem is that once we adopt a particular view of the world, we are not likely to question it.

But sometimes people do begin to question basic beliefs, and when this happens, their emotional lives can change quite radically. How often have you heard someone say, "That situation really used to bother me, but since I changed my outlook on it, I don't get upset about it anymore"? Or how often have you wondered afterward why you got upset over a minor frustration that was "not that big a thing"? The situation that you reacted to has not changed, but your appraisal of it has. If you had appraised it the same way then as now, you would not have become unduly upset. The fact is that the most effective way to influence feelings is to influence the viewpoints that underlie appraisals of situations. And the most effective way to prevent negative and self-defeating emotions is to help your child avoid the pitfalls of the irrational beliefs that underlie such reactions.

Psychologist Albert Ellis has identified some of the major irrational beliefs behind unhappiness and stress. Three of these irrational beliefs are particularly relevant to stress produced by fear of failure:

1. To be worthwhile, one should be thoroughly competent, adequate, and achieving in all possible respects.

2. It is a dire necessity to be loved or approved of by virtually every person in one's life.

3. It is terrible, awful, and catastrophic when things (we, others, the world) are not the way we demand they be.

Now, on first glance, these ideas may seem so extreme as to be nonsensical to you. Most people do not walk around saying things such as these to themselves or to others. Nevertheless, these ideas are reinforced by the culture in which we live, and many people tend to carry them around in their subconscious with little awareness of how these views influence their feelings and behaviors. Ideas such as these would have to be present for people to become terribly upset and anxious about the possibility of performing poorly in a situation that really doesn't matter in the long term; to become upset and depressed when someone who doesn't really matter disapproves of or slights them; or to react to a minor frustration as if it were a true catastrophe. Research has shown that people who have these kinds of emotional reactions do indeed tend to think as if these ideas were correct and rational.

The fear of failure that underlies athletic stress is understandable in a culture such as ours, which emphasizes achievement as a measure of personal worth. In our society untold numbers of children also fall victim to their parents' demands that they perform exactly as expected — and to condemnations when they fail. Too often, the child's achievements are viewed as an indication of the worth of his or her parents, and failure brings reprisals based on the parents' feelings of guilt that they are to blame or that they themselves are inadequate. For many children love becomes a premium handed out on the basis of what a child can *do* rather than simply who he or she is. The fastest and easiest way to create fear of failure in a child is to punish unsuccessful performance by criticizing it or by withholding love from the youngster.

Under such circumstances children learn to dread failure because it is associated with punishment or rejection and to fear and avoid situations in which they might fail. The unfortunate lesson they learn is that their worth and lovability depend on how well they perform. Instead of trying to achieve to reap the intrinsic rewards of achievement and mastery, children strive to perform well to avoid failure. They begin to measure themselves by their performance; and if the latter is inadequate, they usually consider their total being inadequate. A child can ultimately become so fearful of failing that all attempts to succeed are abandoned. This almost guarantees that the child cannot meet the standards he or she has set, and it serves only to reinforce feelings of inadequacy.

One important benefit of sport is that the consequences of failure are temporary and unlikely to influence realistically the future of a child (as failing in school might). Therefore, sports can be a fine training ground for helping your child develop a healthy philosophy about achievement and an ability to tolerate failure when it occurs.

Several things can be done to aid this process: Emphasize to your young athlete that various games and activities in life are enjoyable for the playing, whether you win or lose. Try to raise your child to enjoy many activities in and of themselves so that winning is not a condition for enjoyment. Teach your child that anything worth achieving is rarely easy and that there is nothing disgraceful about it being a long and difficult process to master something. Stress that mistakes, rather than being things to avoid at all costs, can serve as stepping-stones to success. Point out that becoming the best athlete he or she can become is not an achievement to be had merely for the asking, but that practice, practice, and still more practice are needed to master any sport.

As we have recommended throughout the book, emphasize and praise effort as well as outcome. Through your actions and your words, show your child that he or she is just as important to you when trying and failing as when succeeding. If maximum effort is acceptable to you, it can also become acceptable to your young athlete. Above all, do not punish or withdraw love and approval from your child when he or she doesn't perform up to expectations. It is such punishment that builds fear of failure.

Children should be taught not to confuse worth with performance. Impress upon your child that striving for perfection is fine as long as it relates to performance and not to self. Help your youngster to distinguish what she does from what she is. A valuable lesson for children to learn is never to identify their worth as people with any particular part of themselves, such as their school performance, their competence at sports, or their physical appearance. You can further this process by showing your own ability to accept your child unconditionally as a person even when you're communicating that you don't approve of some behavior. Also, show your child that you can gracefully accept your own mistakes and failures, and comment that as a fallible human being you can accept the fact that despite your best efforts, you are going to occasionally bungle things. If your child can learn from you to accept and like himself, he will not unduly require the approval of others to feel worthwhile.

Finally, help your young athlete not to let desires to perform well become dire needs. When we translate our preferences into necessities, we tend to view our failure to get what we want or to do as we would like as catastrophic and to respond with intense emotion. Problems in achievement arise not when youngsters try to do well but when they insist that they do perfectly well — *the* best instead of *their* best. Children who fall into this trap can only accept and value themselves as people when they do remarkably well in their performance. Anything less than near-impossible standards of perfection are reacted to as a catastrophe.

When children learn to enjoy sports for their own sake, when their goal becomes to do their best rather than the best, and when they avoid the trap of defining their self-worth in terms of their performance or the approval of others, then their way of viewing themselves and their world is one that helps prevent stress. Such children are success-oriented rather than failure-oriented. They strive to succeed rather than try to avoid failure. Parents who impart these lessons to their young athletes give them a priceless gift that will benefit them in many of their endeavors in life. There are few areas in a child's life which offer as many opportunities to help him or her develop an adaptive philosophy as sports can.

Controlling Arousal: Teaching Your Child Relaxation Skills

Without carefully examining our thought processes, we may have little awareness of the appraisals that we are making about situations that produce stress. But we are all painfully aware of the physical responses of our bodies to such appraisals. We respond to perceived threat by shifting into high gear on a physiological level. Our heartbeat becomes faster and stronger so that more oxygen can be pumped through our bloodstream to the muscles. Our muscles become tense in readiness to confront the emergency. Stress hormones pouring into our bloodstream increase our level of arousal. These and other physiological changes are experienced by us as the stirred-up state that we associate with emotion. As noted earlier, a moderate level of arousal can psych us up to perform more efficiently. On the other hand, high levels of arousal can interfere with our thought and behavior patterns.

Arousal can be controlled with relaxation training. The ability to remain calm in a stressful situation, or at least to prevent arousal from climbing out of control, is a useful stress-management skill. Many people have found that they can learn to prevent or control tension through training in muscle-relaxation skills. Because one cannot be relaxed and tense at the same time, voluntary relaxation gives us the ability to turn off or tone down tension. Although it is clearly a skill and must be learned through work and practice, most people can train themselves to relax.

Relaxation training actually provides two benefits. The first is the ability to reduce arousal, but the second is equally important. In the course of relaxation training, people become more sensitive to what is going on inside their bodies and are better able to detect arousal in its beginning stages. When we can detect the early warning signals of developing tension, we can plug in our coping responses at an early stage before the tension gets out of control.

Children as young as five or six years of age can be trained in relaxation skills, and they can then use these skills to reduce tension and anxiety. Mastering coping skills at an early age can benefit a child throughout life. Our experience has been that children who learn this and other stress-coping skills show a marked increase in self-confidence and are less reluctant to tackle difficult situations.

We would like to outline a training program that you can use to train your young athlete (and yourself if you wish) in relaxation skills. The approach that we use involves training through a process of voluntarily tensing and relaxing various muscle groups of the body. The goal is to learn voluntary-relaxation skills while gaining increased sensitivity to bodily tension states. We find that within about a week of conscientious training, most people can increase, sometimes dramatically, their ability to relax their bodies and reduce tension.

If you wish to help your young athlete learn relaxation, we recommend that you go through the exercises on your own several times to become familiar with the procedure. Then you can easily guide your youngster through the exercises until he or she becomes familiar enough with them to practice without your help.

We recommend that the relaxation exercises be practiced at least once and preferably twice a day until they are mastered. Practice should be carried out in a comfortable chair. We use a reclining chair to train our clients.

The exercises involve tensing fully and in sequence the major muscles of the body while concentrating total attention on the level of tension. After holding the full tension for five seconds, slowly let the tension out halfway and hold for an additional five seconds. As the tension is slowly released, concentrate carefully on the sensations in your muscles. After holding the tension at the halfway point, slowly decrease it the rest of the way and relax the muscles completely. After the muscles are completely relaxed, focus on deepening the relaxation by giving yourself the mental command to relax each time you exhale during your normal breathing pattern. In this manner the command to relax becomes associated with a relaxed muscular state.

In our training procedure, we start by concentrating on the hands and arms; move to the legs, stomach and chest, back muscles, and neck and jaw; and finish up with the facial and scalp muscles. Here are the steps:

1. While sitting comfortably, bend your arms at the elbow. Now make a hard fist with both hands, and bend your wrists downward while simultaneously tensing the muscles of your upper arms. This will produce a state of tension in your hands, forearms, and upper arms. Hold this tension for five seconds and study it carefully, then slowly let the tension out halfway while concentrating on the sensations in your arms and fingers as tension decreases. Hold the tension at the halfway point for five seconds, and then slowly let the tension out the rest of the way and rest your arms comfortably in your lap. Concentrate carefully on the contrast between the tension which you have just experienced and the relaxation which deepens as you voluntarily relax the muscles for an additional ten to fifteen seconds. As you breathe normally, concentrate on those muscles and give yourself the mental command to relax each time you exhale. Do this for seven to ten breaths. If you train your young athlete, here is a sample of how you can phrase the instructions when presenting this exercise:

We're going to start out with the arms and hands. What I'd like you to do while keeping your eyes closed is to bend your arms and make a fist like this. [*Demonstrate.*] Now make a hard fist and tense those muscles in your arms hard. Notice the tension and the pulling throughout your arm as those muscles stretch and bunch up like rubber bands. Focus on those feelings of tension in your arms and hands.

[*After five seconds*]: Now slowly begin to let that tension out halfway, and concentrate very carefully on the feeling in your arms and hands as you do that. Now hold the tension at the halfway point and notice how your arms and hands are less tense than before but that there is still tension present.

[*After five seconds*]: Now slowly let the tension out all the way and just let your arms and hands become completely relaxed, just letting go and becoming more and more relaxed, feeling all the tension draining away as the muscles let go and become completely relaxed. And now, each time you breathe out, let your mind tell your body to relax, and concentrate on relaxing the muscles even more. That's good . . . just let go.

2. Tense the calf and thigh muscles in your legs. You can do this by straightening out your legs hard while pointing your toes downward. Hold the tension for five seconds, then slowly let it out halfway. Hold at the halfway point for an additional five seconds, and then slowly let the tension out all the way and concentrate on relaxing the muscles as completely as possible. Again, pay careful attention to the feelings of tension and relaxation as they develop. Finish by giving the muscles the mental command "Relax" each time you exhale (seven to ten times), and concentrate on relaxing them as deeply as possible.

3. Cross the palms of your hands in front of your chest and press them together to tense the chest and shoulder muscles. At the same time, tense your stomach muscles hard. As before, hold the tension for five seconds, then slowly let the tension out halfway and focus on the decreasing levels of tension as you do so. Hold again for five seconds at the halfway point and then slowly let the tension out completely. Again, do the breathing procedure with the mental command to deepen the relaxation in your stomach, chest, and shoulder muscles.

4. Arch your back and push your shoulders back as far as possible to tense your upper and lower back muscles. (Be careful not to tense these muscles too hard.) Repeat the standard procedure of slowly releasing the tension halfway, then all the way. Finish by doing the breathing exercise and mental command as you relax your back muscles as deeply as possible.

5. Tense your neck and jaw muscles by thrusting your jaw outward and drawing the corners of your mouth back. Release the tension slowly to the halfway point, hold for five seconds there, and then slowly release the tension in these muscles all the way. Let your head droop into a comfortable position and your jaw slacken as you concentrate on totally relaxing these muscles with your breathing exercise and mental command. (You can also tense your neck muscles in other ways, such as bending your neck forward, backward, or to one side. Experiment to find the way that's best for you. Tense your jaw at the same time.)

6. Wrinkle your forehead and scalp upward to tense these muscles. Hold the tension for five seconds, then release it halfway for an additional five seconds. Then relax your eyes completely. Focus on relaxing your facial and scalp muscles completely, and use your breathing exercise and mental command.

7. While sitting in a totally relaxed position, take a series of short inhalations, about one per second, until your chest is filled and tense. Hold each for about five seconds, then exhale slowly while thinking silently to yourself, "Relax." Most people can produce a deeply relaxed state by doing this. Repeat this exercise three times.

8. Finish off your relaxation practice by concentrating on breathing comfortably into your abdomen (rather than into your chest area). Simply let your stomach fill with air as you inhale, and deepen your relaxation as you exhale. Abdominal breathing is far more relaxing than breathing into the chest.

As you guide your young athlete through the exercises, you can practice them yourself. You will find relaxation very useful in your own life. It not only serves as a weapon against tension and stress, but it produces an enjoyable state in its own right.

Be sure to communicate to your child the reasons for relaxation training before you begin the program. Urge your child to use relaxation skills whenever he or she begins to feel unduly tense. Relaxation can also be used for preparing to deal with stressful situations by imagining these situations while concentrating on remaining completely relaxed. For example, the young athlete might imagine shooting a crucial free throw in a basketball game as vividly as possible while maintaining as deep a state of relaxation as possible. Relaxation together with mental rehearsal is a technique used by many champion athletes as part of their mental preparations for stressful athletic situations. We have found that child athletes can also benefit from this procedure.

The stresses of athletic competition must be faced by all athletes, young and old. As a parent, you can use these stresses as opportunities to teach your youngster coping skills that will be beneficial not only in sports but in other areas of life as well. The athlete's greatest enemy is fear of failure, and anything that you can do to prevent this from developing or to teach your youngster to master it will help to make sport participation more enjoyable and productive.

9

Your Daughter in Sports

Consider this scenario, recently witnessed at a high school basketball tournament:

Karen, an attractive high school student, approaches the foul line with eight seconds to play in the semifinal game of the state high school girls' basketball tournament. Her team trails by one point. If she makes the free throw she ties the game and gives her team the opportunity to go to the championship game. The ball goes up and through the basket, but the referee's whistle blows. The basket doesn't count because Karen's foot had moved across the foul line. The ball goes back to the other team and in seconds the game is over. Karen's team has lost.

The winners are, of course, ecstatic. But Karen walks off the court slowly, unable to hold back her tears. Her boyfriend rushes to her side and, oblivious to the thousands in the stands, hugs her and tries to console her. Karen thinks she will never forget this disappointing day.

Indeed, Karen will always remember her experience, but not just because her team lost. In time, what will be the sharpest in her memory will be the positive feelings of being a team member and belonging; of being part of the best team in the region and district and getting to the state tournament; of playing among champions; and of sharing the experience with her boyfriend.

There is nothing that has contributed more to the fitness, health, and quality of life of young women in America during the last quarter of this century than their acceptance of and into more active life styles of sport participation. Sports bring no fewer benefits to girls than they have traditionally provided boys in every society. Young women have rid themselves of the social restraint of Grandmother's day, when "horses can sweat, men will perspire, but women should only glow."

Today's preadolescent or elementary school–aged girl finds abundant opportunities in most communities for youth sport participation. The goals of sport programs for girls are no different than they are for boys: to provide fun and an opportunity for energy-expending exercise and to introduce girls to a variety of sports and some low-key instruction in sport skills. A proper social environment and attention to suitable sport goals should create for young girls a positive introduction to sports directed toward the lifelong fitness benefits of continued sport participation.

The preadolescent girl has the same physical potential for sport performance as the preadolescent boy. Both possess essentially the same size and strength until approximately age eleven, when the average young girl begins to experience the physical changes of early adolescence. Prior to age eleven, there is no physical reason why most boys and girls should not compete against one another and be on the same teams. But after this age, boys and girls should be directed into their own separate sport programs and competitions, due to rapid but varying changes in their size and strength.

Some argue that if a girl in junior or senior high school is a good enough athlete, she should be allowed on the boys' team. If this argument is valid, then boys who are good athletes should also be allowed to play on girls' teams. Obviously, the bigger and stronger adolescent males would gain almost all the positions on both teams, and the possibility of women participating equally in sports programs would be lost. Therefore, we feel that separate sports teams and competitions are best after puberty.

Prior to high school years, American football, ice hockey, wrestling, and other collision sports are not particularly suitable—for boys or girls. It seems best not to encourage elementary school–aged girls and preadolescent girls (even though they are at no physical disadvantage to boys) to participate in the sports that become men's sports later on. They can provide no particular benefit for preadolescent girls, and a variety of other sport experiences is more apt to satisfy the goals of the younger girl.

There is a variety of sports that are suitable for the early experience of younger girls, including soccer, softball, swimming, track and field, skiing, and tennis. All can be very positive introductions to active sport participation when the goals and objectives of the sport experience for this age group are kept clearly in mind. As with the programs of elementary school–aged boys, girls' sport programs should have the primary goal of providing fun and enjoyment. In addition to fun the well-oriented sport program for the grade school girl should provide an opportunity for important energy-expending exercises. Since the typical American child of this age watches more than four hours of television every weekday, anything that directs the child away from that mesmerizing, sedentary activity into physical exercise will be beneficial. The early youth sport experience can and should be an interesting introduction into one or more sports and the start of early development of some sport skills. The preadolescent will not have the maturity of the nervous system or of muscles—the strength, coordination, or endurance—to become very proficient in sport skills. Early coaching and instruction in sport skills should be low-key. Ribbons, trophies, and medals in sports at this early age are more for the participating adults — parents and coaches — than for the young athletes.

Sports and the Early Adolescent Girl: The Eleven- to Fifteen-Year-Old

For the average young girl, life begins to take on some interesting new perspectives soon after her eleventh birthday. Quite suddenly she begins to look and feel different. Her relationship with her mother is more complex and even her father doesn't roughhouse and treat her as he always has. The boys at school are absolutely ridiculous, and in the midst of all this, friends and belonging become the most important thing in life. It is not difficult to understand why a junior or senior high school sport experience can be a highly prized one for a girl during early and later adolescence and why women's sports have enjoyed an explosion in popularity during the past decade.

In sports there is the opportunity to test and compare the newly developing physique and to experience the physical well-being that comes from regular exercise. Most important, of course, is the acceptance and security that comes from making the team. Recently several thousand junior and senior high school boys and girls were asked to give a stress rating to a long list of stressful experiences that could be encountered during the high school years. Failure to be successful in some peer-related activity ranked very near the top of the list.

Failure to make the team can be a source of considerable anxiety. The adolescent girl recognizes during this period of change how reassuring it is to have the acceptance, the new friends, and the demonstrated adequacy that comes from making the team. By fourteen or fifteen years of age, the young athlete is not as threatened by losing a game or contest as she might have been as a preadolescent. Now, however, failure to make the team becomes a very dominant concern. This development is true for both boys and girls at this age.

Sport participation can be a particularly positive experience for the late-maturing girl. In contrast to the sports enjoyed by males, women's sports are not so dependent on muscle strength and body weight. Thus, the late-maturing girl whose jeans and T-shirt can't be filled out nearly as well as her classmates' may very well be able to run faster, jump higher, and throw a ball better. Today these talents can give her a place in the sports arena early on. In the past the very tall, late-maturing junior and senior high school girl often had less access to the mainstream of the most popular school activities. Women's basketball and volleyball have provided an especially welcome haven for the very tall adolescent who will almost always be a late maturer.

There can be too much, too soon for girls, too. The twelve- to fourteen-year-old female will often be physically capable of training for elite performance in many women's sports. The size and strength that come with full maturity may not be as essential for world-class performance in many women's sports as it is in many men's sports. Thus, young girls could be led into striving toward goals that are unrealistic, given only average innate ability. Elite athletes are born; they are not created out of common clay simply by hard training, the best coaching, or the most eager parents. All too many young girls have sacrificed academic accomplishments and maturing social experiences during much of their adolescence only to admit finally that a national- or world-class performance in gymnastics, figure skating, or swimming was not to be theirs.

It is not uncommon to encounter the young high school woman athlete who is hiding from normal maturing opportunities and responsibilities in her intense commitment to a sport program. Initially encouraged by parents and coaches, she lets the commitment get out of hand with excessive training schedules of endless hours in the gym or miles of running. The inevitable result is weight loss, confusion, depression, and a deterioration of what perhaps never was truly outstanding sport performance. This call for help should be recognized for what it is and should prompt control of athletic activities and, if necessary, counseling.

One result of the great increase in sport participation by girls and young women in recent years is that not even the most vigorous athletic training is looked upon as unfeminine. The active preadolescent girl in sport is no longer the tomboy of the neighborhood. There is no longer anything unfeminine about playing first base on the softball team or spiking the ball on the volleyball team. Sports participation doesn't make today's young women mannish, but it does provide them a host of social and fitness advantages.

Conditioning and Training for the Female Athlete

Good conditioning is obviously no less important for the girl or young woman than it is for her male counterpart. Being in condition is essential for proficiency in sport, and even more important, it is essential for having fun. Conditioning is particularly important for young women who may be having their first active sport experience in high school or college after a sport-free childhood. These young women have muscles, ligaments, and other body structures that need a gradual and well-planned introduction to sport and exercise.

We have found that many young women come to the University of Washington with no previous experience in organized sports. Attracted to new opportunities in women's sports, they show up as candidates for the women's rowing team. Very few men or women have any rowing experience prior to college, and thus these new athletes recognize that they are not at any significant skill disadvantage for not having rowed previously. Rowing is a physically demanding sport, and the early weeks of training involve an intense conditioning effort, with long-distance running, stair running, weight training, stretching, and so on. Candidates for the women's rowing team show up in large numbers at the sport medicine clinic with the entire spectrum of common overuse symptoms: mild muscle strains, tendonitis, stress fractures, shin-splints, and so on. New women athletes at the high school or college level who have no previous sport experience should conscientiously condition themselves in a well-graded program before that first sport season begins.

Preseason training can provide a wonderful opportunity for the junior or senior high school crowd to work out together on an effective schedule. They can have some fun doing what otherwise may become somewhat of a dreary chore. With suggestions from the coach or simply by consulting some well-spelled-out preseason training schedules, prospective athletes and their friends can set up effective programs. Programs involve some aerobic conditioning, with increasing distances of running, bicycling, or swimming; weight training with or without weights; and stretching. It is generally accepted that conditioning workouts three or four times a week will induce desired levels of increased conditioning and fitness. Workouts two to three times a week will maintain good fitness once a desired level is achieved. A well-organized training program need take no longer than an hour a session. With a group of good friends, it can last as long as it's fun.

The first essential of an effective training program is to begin early. This beginning can be at least a month or six weeks before the sport season starts, when the athlete competes for a place on the team. Second, take it easy! Going too hard too fast only produces injuries that keep the athlete out of participation. Avoid pain! You should know that anytime a joint or muscle hurts, you are hurting it. Getting in the best of condition for sports can demand some hard work and effort; but contrary to certain popular slogans heard around the gym, it does not demand pain.

An essential in any conditioning program is determining a desired level of body fatness and body weight for competition and achieving it before the season begins. A nutrition and exercise program to achieve and maintain competing weight is discussed in the chapter on nutrition. But again, as with other aspects of training, begin early. Rapid reductions in body fat are incompatible with good performances in sport, in school, or in just getting through the day.

Nutrition Concerns

Another important benefit enjoyed by millions of women and young girls who are new to sport is the solution they have found to the nutrition fitness crisis of American women. This became a prominent problem among populations of women in industrialized nations, especially the United States, during the 1950s and 1960s. Society became obsessed with the thinness of women. To be fat was inexcusable, unacceptable, and a social handicap. At the same time as the sylphlike figure was accepted as the desired body form, women became part of the highly mechanized, low-energy-expending population of post–World War II America. There appeared the second car, the escalator, the school bus, the gadgetized household, the television, and an endless list of power-driven devices that even took energy expenditure out of recreation and leisure time. Finding it essentially impossible to get any energy-expending exercise and faced with the absolute necessity of staying as thin as possible, American women became chronic dieters and calorie counters. Food intake often had to be so minuscule to avoid obesity that intake of essential nutrients bordered on the inadequate. This was especially true of young females during their growing years. After an extensive government-sponsored investigation into the nutrition status of this country's population in the late 1960s, it was concluded that the population at greatest nutrition-related health risk was females in junior and senior high school.

Daughters in middle- and upper-income families were found to be at particular risk because of intense pressure to be thin, reliance on the automobile, and the money to buy snack-food lunches rather than subsidized, nutritious school lunches.

During this period schools did not provide many opportunities for the sport participation of female students. Young women in high school could lead cheers, serve as pompom girls, sit on committees, or participate in music organizations.

In the 1970s, women and men began to discover the fun and fitness benefits of sport participation and exercise. Millions began to jog and run, play tennis, bicycle, ski, frequent racketball courts, and demand that schools, colleges, and universities provide facilities for sport participation for both women and men. Assisted by legislation (Title IX) and with continuing interest on the part of ever-increasing numbers of young people and adults alike, athletic programs continued to grow. Women began to eat better and increase intake of essential nutrients, yet decrease their risk of being overweight.

During the past ten years, better health and fitness have been documented repeatedly in populations of women athletes. Active athletes eat generous diets to provide the energy needed for their training. Such generous, mixed diets are more apt to provide the essential nutrients they need, such as iron. For example, women in varsity athletic programs at the University of Washington have a frequency of inadequate iron intake of not more than 6 percent, whereas the nonathletic population of similar education and economic status has an incidence of more than 20 percent. Fat women don't stay overweight very long if they participate in a varsity sport program. Less sophisticated athletes—the recreational runner or regular tennis player—can enjoy similar nutrition and fitness benefits through regular energy-expending exercise. There is no way that a young woman can enjoy a high level of nutrition-related good health without regular exercise.

Food and diet needs of male and female athletes differ in only a few specifics. Both need sufficient intake of food and water throughout the day to maintain desired competing weights. Although women sweat less than men, they tolerate exercise in heat as well as men, compensating for less-effective sweat production with a greater sweat loss through a greater skin surface (in relation to body weight). However, water loss can remain a problem. Most women and girls are not nearly as inclined to drink water as men, perhaps because they are less accustomed to the requirements of sport competition. Adequate fluid intake is essential for both performance and safety.

Iron is an essential nutrient and has recently been shown to be of real concern to the female athlete. The only normal mechanisms the human body has for losing any significant amounts of body iron are through menstruation, pregnancy, and birth. Only through abnormal blood losses will males ever lose such significant amounts of iron. Both men and women need iron in their diets for growth and repair of body tissues. The female has an additional iron requirement to satisfy the varying needs of menstruation and pregnancy.

In a recent Swedish study of a population of very healthy young women, there was more than a tenfold variation in the amount of iron lost in each menstrual cycle. Each of the subjects in the study was very consistent in the amount of menstrual iron loss she experienced each month. Some individuals needed consistently little iron from their diets (actually little more than a male of similar size), whereas others had much greater iron needs. Inasmuch as all young females eat roughly similar diets and do not modify their dietary intake to their menstrual experience, a certain segment of a healthy population of young women is expected to be at increased risk to failing to meet iron needs. The result, of course, is a nutritional deficiency of iron. National nutrition surveys have documented during the past decade that roughly 20 percent of women in middle- and upper-income families and as many as 50 percent of women in poverty circumstances fail to satisfy their dietary needs for iron and are iron-deficient to some degree. Some, but not nearly all, will be depleted to such an extent and for such a period that they will be noticeably anemic. The fact that large numbers of women fail to take in sufficient iron to meet their needs is assuming new importance, since researchers have demonstrated that degrees of iron deficiency not severe enough to cause anemia actually do cause a variety of symptoms. This is a particular concern for a woman in sport who is at risk to iron depletion.

One of the most significant of the recent studies in iron deficiency found that nonanemic iron-depleted rats trained to run on a treadmill were unable to run as long as their counterparts with good levels of iron in their tissues. The study also demonstrated that the body chemistry involved in the utilization of carbohydrate energy was not able to function normally. These animal studies prompted similar studies of high-performing women athletes from the University of Washington varsity sports program. By screening the iron status of several hundred varsity athletes, researchers found a small number of volunteers who were iron-depleted and others whose iron status was excellent. In the laboratory the iron-depleted subjects fatigued early and underperformed in tests of endurance. Following correction of their iron lack with medicinal supplements, the iron-depleted athletes performed as well as their better-nourished teammates and no longer showed any evidence of limited energy production. Studies of iron-depleted animals have shown altered thyroid-hormone function, cold intolerance, some changes in brain metabolism, and limited energy metabolism. Some of these changes are currently being investigated in human subjects who are iron-depleted but not detectably anemic. There may be a very real public-health concern in what in the past was looked upon as a mild, clinically insignificant iron deficiency.

At present, with a well-documented alteration in the energy metabolism of the iron-depleted but not anemic subject, there appears to be a prudent need to assess the iron status of young women who are beginning to make a serious commitment to sport participation or those who for unexplained reasons experience a significant deterioration in their athletic performance and endurance. Because the early stages of iron depletion do not result in lowered blood hemoglobin to an extent sufficient to cause anemia, merely checking blood hemoglobin levels will not effectively screen for the iron problem. A physician should be consulted. The physician will have access to appropriate biochemical measures of iron status, such as plasma ferritin determination or transferrin saturation test. In light of recent research findings, such a biochemical screening test will probably someday be recommended for all young women a few years after their menstrual pattern of blood loss and iron requirement has been established. Such a test could identify very early those women whose perfectly normal menstrual iron losses are greater than average and whose iron need cannot be met with the iron available in even a good-quality American diet.

A reasonable response of those now aware of the importance of the iron problem might seem to be not to worry about getting a laboratory assessment of iron status, but to begin to take iron just to be safe. Such an approach to the iron problem is very ill advised. First, the vast majority of young women do not need a supplement. Second, if there indeed are iron-depleted young women in the sports program, it is essential that the precise cause of their iron lack be identified and that they receive adequate iron treatment, which can only be obtained by prescription under the supervision of a physician.

Some Sport Concerns for Women Only

Menstruation

With the marked increase in sports participation by young women, there is a very natural concern about the effect of menstruation on sport performance as well as about the impact of intense competition and training on a young woman's reproductive cycle.

Limited studies to date suggest that with the exception of swimmers, the age of menarche (the onset of the menstrual period) is later in women athletes than in nonathletes. A study of 145 female athletes at the Montreal Olympic Games found that the average age of onset of menses was 13.7 years and that women athletes had a later onset than did the general population of their country of origin. Runners and gymnasts as groups had the latest onset — 14.3 and 14.5 years — and swimmers had the earliest, 13.1 years. In another investigation the onset of the menstruation was found to be 14.2 years in a group of Olympic volleyball players, 13 years in high school and college athletes, and 12.2 years in a matched population of nonathletes. The reason for the delayed onset of menstruation in athletes is not well defined and doubtless varies in different populations of women. In some the stress of intense training and competition at an early age may delay the onset of menstruation. In others, such as gymnasts and long-distance runners, the marked reduction in the level of body fat for elite performance could be a factor. In sports such as basketball and volleyball, very tall girls become elite performers. To attain an extremely tall height, most girls experience a prolonged period of preadolescent growth and are late maturers. The late onset of menstruation is part of their slower-than-average maturation process.

The relation of menstrual flow to sport performance has been investigated in several populations of elite athletes. Olympic gold medals have been won by women during every phase of the menstrual cycle. Elite athletes report that they train and compete without difficulty during and between periods. For whatever reason, disabling menstrual-related discomfort is less common in athletes. Dealing with menstrual discomfort in sport performance, training, and competing depends on the severity of the pain and the degree of commitment of the young woman to her sport program. A physician can prescribe medications that are quite effective in providing symptomatic relief for the discomfort experienced by many and that will permit continued training or competition. If the discomfort makes sport participation painful and unpleasant, the young female athlete should remain on the sidelines temporarily. It isn't necessary to prove anything by ignoring the body's signals.

Although there are fewer problems of menstrual irregularity and discomfort among athletes than nonathletes, the incidence of missed periods and the cessation of the menstrual cycle for prolonged periods occur commonly in populations of those athletes who are involved in intense training. Those young women most likely to experience missed periods and interruption of the normal menstrual cycle include distance runners and other endurance athletes who experience marked reductions in their level of body fat; those making a very keen commitment to a given period of training; those who had a late menarche; and any girls who experienced irregular menstrual periods before beginning sport participation and training.

The long-term effects of irregular menstrual cycles and missed periods on women's health and reproductive capacity are not known. Anecdotal reports of several elite athletes who have experienced altered menstrual function with training and sport participation but normal pregnancies suggest that there is no evidence of any decreased fertility. Women athletes reportedly experience fewer complications of pregnancy, fewer Caesarean sections, shorter duration of labor, and fewer spontaneous abortions; this is not an unexpected reproductive record for a population of very fit women. For the young female athlete who is intensely involved in sport and is experiencing irregular menstrual periods, prolonged periods, or absence of menstrual cycles, a visit to the gynecologist is strongly recommended.

Equipment Needs of the Female Athlete

With the wonderful expansion in the number of women and girls participating in sports and the great variation in the sports they are involved in, there are certain needs for better equipment for the female athlete. In most situations female sports equipment, such as shoes, socks, shorts, pants, sweatshirts, and jerseys, is no different from that of the male athlete. All equipment should be clean and in good repair and should fit properly. This is obviously of considerable importance in regard to footwear. Proper-fitting jerseys can become important if there is underlying protective padding that must be held in place by a good-fitting jersey.

Hot weather presents a unique challenge to the woman athlete who can't go topless to expose heat-radiating skin as her male counterpart can. Cutoffs — half-tops exposing the lower chest and upper abdomen — are appropriate pieces of equipment for distance runners and other athletes who may train and compete in warm and humid weather.

Attention must be given to the problem of support and protection of the female breast in vigorous sport activities. Being a quite freely mobile fatty structure, the female breast is not very vulnerable to significant injury. Serious bruises requiring surgery have occurred in a few rare instances in which the breasts, firmly immobilized against the chest with a wide elastic bandage, received a strong blow. With excellent breast-support bras available for the active athlete, there is no reason to support and immobilize the breasts in this inappropriate manner. There is no evidence to suggest that bumps or bruises in a well-supported breast during athletic participation will have any relation to the eventual development of cancer or tumors.

Presently there are on the market a few well-designed bras, such as the sports bra manufactured by Lily of France, for the female athlete. One bra that can be highly recommended was designed after very sophisticated biomechanical research by a group of investigators headed by Christine Haycock, a surgeon and accomplished athlete. This bra, marketed as the Lady Duke, is an excellent support for the breast and can even be padded for protection in sports in which padding may be desired. Good support of the breasts during active body movements is essential for comfort and good performance.

The female athlete may pursue sports that warrant special equipment attention. Some sports require strength training on certain popular pieces of equipment that have been designed for use by adult males. Young males and most females do not fit these pieces of training equipment and should use them with discretion if injuries and overuse problems are to be avoided. Also, some athletes exercise on seats designed for use by males. The dimensions of the pelvic bones on which women sit differ greatly from men's. The seats of racing or touring bicycles, of racing shells, and of white-water kayaks all may be sources of considerable discomfort to the female athlete. Seats designed for women in these sports can be specially ordered. They provide a good bit of comfort to the female and improve her performance.

10

What? You Want Me to Coach?

Gregg Caswell looked stunned as he hung up the telephone. "I don't believe what I just did."

"What was that all about?" asked his wife, Laurie.

"That was Elmer Hendley, the head of the coed softball league that Angie's been playing in. He called with this hard-luck story about how they're short of coaches and that they're considering reducing the number of teams this year. I knew what was coming when he said that Angie's been playing for three years now and that he's seen us at a lot of games. Well, to make a long story short, I let him talk me into coaching one of the teams. I can see why Elmer's insurance business is so successful. Now what am I going to do? I've never coached fifteen kids before and don't know where to begin."

Laurie laughed. "It looks like you're in for a long season."

"You won't be so amused when I tell you the rest. The team also needs an assistant coach and Elmer said you'd be perfect. So you're it."

Is this scene straight out of one of your nightmares? What would you do in Gregg and Laurie's place? The fact is that many volunteer coaches become involved in precisely this way and have the same reservations about their abilities to coach. But programs could not exist without adults who are willing to give their time and energies to coaching youngsters.

Coaches Are Very Important People

If you are a youth sport coach, you are among the estimated 2.5 million adults in the United States who supervise children's sports. Approximately 60 percent of these are parents themselves.

Coaches occupy a central and critical role in the youth sport setting. In fact, the nature of the relationship between coach and player is a primary determinant of the ways participation in organized athletic programs ultimately affect the lives of children. Not only do coaches occupy a key position in sports, but their influence can extend into other areas of children's lives as well. For the many children from single-parent families, coaches may occupy the role of a substitute parent, with enormous potential for a positive impact. The manner in which coaches structure the athletic situation, the goal priorities they establish, and the way in which they relate to their players can greatly influence the outcome

of participation. Coaches should never underestimate their importance in the lives of their young athletes.

If you are not a coach, do you have aspirations to become one?
Why not seriously consider devoting some of your time and energy
to this very worthwhile activity? Many potential coaches hesitate
to volunteer; they don't know enough, they think, or they have
never been star athletes. This is understandable. Most people tend
to shy away from things they have little training for or experience
with. However, if you truly want to, you can acquire the necessary
knowledge and skills to become a successful coach and an
important person in the lives of some young athletes. Your
contributions will be appreciated.

If you are not a coach and don't wish to become one, don't skip
this chapter! The information that follows concerns basic psychological principles for any leadership role (including parenting), and
knowledge of these principles will help you to evaluate the coaches
in any sports program your child might participate in.

Sport Psychology Goes to the Ball Park

This book does not deal with how to teach sports skills. There is
an abundance of instructional materials on teaching techniques and
strategies for various sports. Also, coaching clinics that teach sports
skills and training programs for athletes are available.

But a qualified coach must understand more than the mechanics
of sports. He or she must be able to create a healthy psychological
environment for young athletes — an environment that fosters
athletic, personal, and social development. In this chapter we
explore the psychological relationship between coaches and their
players. We describe specific ways in which coaches can use this
relationship to increase the value of sports participation. We give
emphasis to techniques that are taught in a sport psychology
training program for coaches (called Coach Effectiveness Training,
or CET) in many parts of the United States and Canada. The
techniques described here are specifically designed to improve
psychological relations between youth coaches and their athletes.

Unlike many aspects of coaching, CET is based on scientific
evidence rather than on athletic folklore. Over a seven-year period
we carried out a two-phase research project supported by the
National Institute of Mental Health. In phase 1, a large-scale study

was done to determine how specific coaching behaviors influenced players' attitudes toward their coach, teammates, and themselves. We also studied how characteristics of the children, such as their age and level of self-esteem, affected their responses to specific coaching styles.

Phase 2 used the research results of phase 1 to develop our psychologically oriented training program. To test the effectiveness of the program, one group of coaches participated in a CET workshop, serving as an experimental group. They were compared with a group of coaches who did not receive any special training. We observed how the two groups of coaches behaved, and we measured the sport-related attitudes and self-esteem of the youngsters who played for them.

The results were quite encouraging. Careful observations showed that the behavior of trained coaches was much more in agreement with the guidelines than was the behavior of the coaches who had not received the training. The experimental coaches not only learned the guidelines, they applied them. Despite the fact that the average won-lost records of the two groups of coaches were similar, trained coaches were liked better and were rated better teachers by their players.

The positive psychological climate created by the trained coaches had other effects as well. The players of the trained coaches liked the other members of their team more, and they showed stronger feelings of self-esteem. Those children low in preseason self-esteem showed large increases in self-esteem when playing for the trained coaches. They liked their experience, their coach, their teammates, and themselves better.

CET began by conducting workshops with Little League Baseball coaches, but is now being offered for other sports, such as soccer, football, basketball, wrestling, and hockey. Groups of coaches in youth organizations, such as the Boys Clubs of America, the Girls Clubs of America, the Young Men's Christian Association, the United States Soccer Federation, and the Catholic Youth Organization, also participate in CET.

Relating to Child Athletes: Some Do's and Don'ts

The toughest and most challenging part of coaching is the psychology of getting what you want to teach across to the kids, gaining their respect, and making them feel glad that they played for you. When things click on a psychological level, I find that I really get much more enjoyment out of coaching.

A youth sport coach

As a coach you very clearly are trying to influence children in a number of ways. You want to create a good learning situation so that the youngsters pick up the skills you are trying to teach them. You want to create an enjoyable interpersonal situation in which your players relate well to one another and to you. You also want to provide a setting or an atmosphere in which your players develop positive personality traits. The decisions that you make and things that you do are attempts to influence your players in positive ways. Put very simply, you are trying to increase certain desired behaviors on the part of your players and decrease undesirable behaviors.

What we refer to as the psychology of coaching is simply a set of principles to increase the ability to positively influence others. In the pages to follow, we want to present some psychological principles that you can use to become a more effective coach. Many of these principles will be recognized as things that you already do. There is nothing mystical about them. It is often said that psychology is the application of common sense, and we think that these guidelines make good common sense, in addition to being scientifically valid. The challenging part comes not so much in learning the principles, but in adapting them to your own particular coaching style.

There are two basic approaches to influencing people. One approach, which we call the positive approach, is designed to strengthen desired behaviors by motivating people to perform them. The second approach, the negative approach, attempts to eliminate negative behaviors through punishment and criticism. The motivating factor in the second approach is fear. Both of these approaches are used by coaches, but there are a number of reasons why the positive approach is preferred. First of all, it works much better. Second, it creates an enjoyable climate.

The Importance of Reinforcement and Encouragement

The positive approach to coaching is characterized by liberal use of reinforcement and encouragement. The most effective way to build desirable behaviors is to use the reward power you have as a coach. In our research we found that the single most important difference between those coaches to whom young athletes respond most favorably and those to whom they respond least favorably was the frequency with which coaches reinforced desirable behaviors. Reinforcement can include many things — a pat on the back, a smile, clapping, verbal praise, a friendly nod. Be liberal with reinforcement. Look for the positive things, reinforce them, and you'll see them increase. Praise the little things that others might not notice. Reinforcement, sincerely given, does not spoil people; rather, it gives them something to strive for. Have realistic expectations and consistently reinforce players when they succeed in meeting them. Reinforce positive things as soon as they occur, since immediate reinforcement is more potent. Remember, whether youngsters show it or not, the positive things you say and do stick with them.

What you choose to reinforce is of critical importance. It's easy to recognize and praise a player who has just made a great play. It's less natural to reinforce the player who put forth great effort but did not make the play. Perhaps the second player deserves praise even more. Reinforce effort as much as you do results. Players have complete control over how much effort they make; they have only limited control over the outcome of their efforts. Don't take these efforts for granted; let the players know that you appreciate and value them.

Encouragement is also an important part of the positive approach to coaching. Most players are already motivated to develop their skills and play well. Encouragement helps to increase their natural enthusiasm. Again, encourage effort; don't demand results. Use encouragement selectively so that it means something. Be supportive without acting like a cheerleader.

Never give encouragement in a sarcastic or degrading manner: "Come on, gang, we're only down 37 to 1. Let's really come back and make it 37 to 2." Obviously, encouragement given in this manner increases irritation and frustration in players.

It's important to be realistic and base your encouragement on reasonable expectations. Don't encourage your eight-year-olds to strive for Olympic standards; they may feel like failures when they find they can't reach the goals they think you've set. Again, encouraging effort rather than outcome can help avoid this problem.

Encouragement can become contagious and can build team unity. It helps you communicate the enthusiasm you feel, and this rubs off on others. Try to get your players to be supportive and encouraging of one another. The best way to do this is to be an enthusiastic model and to reward your players when they encourage one another: "Way to go! Let's boost each other up!"

Reacting to Mistakes:
The Positive Sandwich

As much as we enjoy seeing home runs, touchdowns, goals, and all-out effort, much of the time coaches must deal with mistakes, screw-ups, boneheaded plays — all the things that the pros seldom do. How you react to these situations is critically important. If you handle them badly, you risk creating a fear of failure in players that can harm not only their performance but also their outlook on themselves, the sport, and their coach.

Whether they show it or not, most players feel embarrassed when they make a mistake. The most useful thing you can do is to give them encouragement immediately after the mistake. That's when the youngster needs it most. If you manage things right, this can also be a golden opportunity to provide corrective instruction. The player wishes that he or she had done it correctly, and the instruction may be particularly meaningful at that time. A general principle to follow is that if you are sure the player knows how to correct the mistake, then encouragement alone is sufficient. To tell a player what he or she already knows is more irritating than helpful.

If you feel that it will be useful, give corrective instruction, but do it in an encouraging and positive fashion. Emphasize not the bad thing that just happened but good things that will happen if the player follows your instructions (the *why* of it). Your instructions should have three elements, which we term the *positive sandwich*.

1. Start with a compliment. ("Way to hustle. You really ran a good pattern.")

2. Follow this up with the future-oriented corrective instruction. ("If you follow the ball all the way into your hands, you'll snag those.")

3. Then end with another positive statement. ("Hang in there. You're going to get even better if you work hard at it.")

This kind of sandwich, consisting of praise for something done right and an encouraging positive remark wrapped around a constructive suggestion, is apt to make the player feel encouraged as a result of what you've said. Emphasizing the positive things that will happen if he or she follows your instruction will tend to motivate the player to make the good things happen rather than to avoid failure and disapproval.

Even Mistakes Can Have a Positive Side

Most of us tend to focus on the negative side of our and others' mistakes. We regard them as something bad, something to be avoided at all costs. But mistakes do in fact have a positive side. They provide the information that we need to help improve performance and as such are important stepping-stones to achievement. If coaches can communicate this concept to players, they can help them to accept and learn from their mistakes.

There are several don'ts to be mentioned in relation to mistakes. First, don't punish when things go wrong. Punishing statements ("Let me see the bottom of your feet. I thought so, you're growing roots into the field") do little to increase positive motivation. Punishment isn't just yelling; it can be any form of disapproval, whether tone of voice or action. Young athletes respond much better to a positive approach.

A second don't involves giving corrective instruction. Avoid doing so in a punitive or hostile manner. ("How many times do I have to tell you to catch with two hands? Your teeth will thank you.") This kind of negative approach to giving instruction is more likely to increase frustration and create resentment than to improve performance. Don't let your good intentions in giving instruction be self-defeating.

Athletic motivation takes several forms. Many athletes try to achieve because of a positive desire to succeed. Unfortunately, many others are motivated primarily by fear of failure. As we noted in Chapter 2, the positively motivated athlete welcomes and peaks under pressure, while the fear-of-failure youngster dreads critical situations and the possibility of failure and disapproval. If he's in the on-deck circle with two outs, his team down by one run, and runners on second and third, he's likely to mentally say to the batter, "Either strike out or knock them in, but for Pete's sake, don't walk."

Fear of failure can be an athlete's worst enemy. Not only can it harm performance, but it detracts from the enjoyment of competing. It also may keep players from trying and thereby risking failure. Many people never fail in reality, but they do so in their imagination and thus never try.

As a coach there are several things you can do to reduce fear of failure in your players. The positive approach discussed above is designed to create positive motivation rather than fear of failing. In addition, if you can deal honestly and openly with your own mistakes, your players will be better able to accept their mistakes and learn from them. Former UCLA Bruins coach John Wooden once told a group of coaches:

> You must know quite well that you are not perfect, that you're going to make mistakes. But you must not be afraid of making mistakes or you won't do anything, and that's the greatest mistake of all. We must have initiative and act and know that we're going to fail at times, for failure will only make us stronger if we accept it properly.

Maintaining Order and Discipline

At a recent coaching clinic, youth coaches were invited to submit questions about common problems. More than two thirds of their questions had to do with preventing misbehavior during games and practices. This can indeed become a serious problem unless the coach deals with it effectively early in the season.

There are several factors that one should understand about young athletes' behaviors in relation to this problem. First, as we've noted earlier, children are not miniature adults. It is an unusual child who wants to sit still during a vigorous play activity. Second, preadolescents and adolescents are establishing their independence and personal identity, and this can cause them to test the limits imposed by authority figures.

But there is another factor that works in favor of coaches: Youngsters want clearly defined limits and structure. They don't like unpredictability and inconsistency. Coaches can utilize this desire to create a well-defined situation in which athletes can have plenty of freedom and fun within reasonable limits.

Young athletes also want their coach to be a leader, not a policeman. There is a lot of evidence that people are more willing to live by rules when they have had a hand in formulating them and they have made a public commitment to abide by them. While it is your job as a coach to maintain reasonable order and discipline, there are several things you can do to involve your players in the process. With older players, you can introduce the topic at an early team meeting by saying something such as: "I think rules and regulations are an important part of the game, because the game happens to be rules and regulations. Our team rules ought to be something we can agree upon. I have a set of rules that I feel are important. But we all have to follow them, so you ought to think about what *you* want. They should be your rules too." The advantage of this approach is that if the rules are truly team rules, then when someone breaks them, it's not your rules he's breaking, but his own rules.

Obviously, very young children are not in a position to actually develop a set of rules; they're looking to you to do that. But even here, players will follow the rules better if they have been somehow involved. When you discuss your rules, make sure the players understand the reasons for them and how the rules will contribute to making them a better team. Ask the players if they have any suggestions and ideas, and listen to what they say (do not necessarily accept it as policy) to show that you value their ideas and feelings.

Coming up with rules is easier than dealing with violations of them. The most important thing is to be consistent and impartial in dealing with violations. When a violation occurs, don't blow up and express a punitive attitude. Don't lecture or embarrass players. Focus on the fact that they've broken a team policy without degrading them as people or making them feel that they're in your doghouse. Simply remind players that they have violated a rule that they agreed to follow, and because of that (not because of you) they must automatically pay the penalty. This approach focuses the responsibility where it belongs, on the player, and it helps to build a sense of personal accountability and responsibility.

What kinds of penalties should be given out for rules violations? It is best to deprive children of something they value rather than to make them do something aversive. For example, telling a player to sit off to the side ("time out" or "the penalty box") is preferable to making the youngster run laps or do pushups (since we don't want beneficial physical activities to become distasteful by using them as punishment). Remember also to keep the lines of communication open and to allow the child to explain his or her actions. There may be a reasonable cause for what the player did or didn't do.

Rules can play an important role in building team unity. Emphasize that during a game all members of the team are part of the game, especially those on the bench. Use reinforcement to strengthen team participation. In other words, apply the positive approach in this area as well. By strengthening desirable behaviors, you can automatically prevent misbehaviors from occurring. By reinforcing players when they're "in the game" and following team rules, you can increase team unity, which is rewarding in itself.

Creating a Good Learning Atmosphere

> There is nothing mysterious about developing a good team, because coaching is nothing more than teaching. Coaches impart the techniques to the players. The better job they do, the better job the players will do.
>
> John McKay,
> *professional football coach*

Although our focus is not on the teaching of specific sports, we'd like to offer a few general guidelines.

Your players expect you to help them satisfy their desire to become as skilled as possible. Therefore, establish your role as teacher as early as possible. Try to structure participation as a learning (rather than competitive) situation in which you're going to help the youngsters develop their abilities.

The positive approach can be used to increase skill learning. Always give instruction to children in a positive manner, emphasizing the good things that will happen if they do it right rather than focusing on the bad things that will happen if they don't. As we noted earlier, this approach motivates the players to make the good things happen instead of creating fear of making a mistake. Give instructions in a clear, concise manner and, if possible, show the players how to do it correctly. Reinforce effort and progress toward the desired performance. Be patient and don't expect or demand more than maximum effort.

One approach to instruction is to use your more mature and

skilled players to instruct younger players. The teacher-learner relationships that develop can help weld the team. But if you do this, make sure that the player-teachers use the positive approach that we've emphasized. If they don't, they can have a destructive influence.

It's important that during each practice or game, every youngster get recognized at least once. Those players who usually get the most recognition are the stars or those who are causing problems. The average players need attention as well. When coaches are asked to keep a count of how often they talk to each player, they often discover that there are some players who get very little attention. You might try this yourself.

If an athlete has had a bad practice or a rough game (as we all have), that game or practice should not end with the youngster going home feeling badly. He or she should get some kind of support from you, a pat on the back, a kind word. ("Hey, we're going to work that out in practice," or "This must have been a tough day for you. I know what you're going through, but everyone has days like that sometimes.") Don't let your players leave feeling alienated from you or feeling like losers.

Gaining Players' Respect

Treat athletes like they are your family. Your program discipline breeds self-discipline. Love — find something in each player to love them for. Don't spoil them — no special deals or star treatment.

Don James,
former football Coach of the Year

All of what we've emphasized up to now is relevant to gaining the respect of your players. There are two keys to gaining such respect:

1. Show your players that you can teach them to develop their skills and that you're willing to make the effort to do so.

2. Be a fair and considerate leader. Show them that you care about them as individuals and that you're glad to be coaching them.

Set a good example by showing respect for yourself, for them, and for others — opponents, parents, officials. You cannot demand respect. True respect must be earned.

Communicating Effectively

Everything you do communicates something to your players. Develop the habit of asking yourself (and at times your players) what your actions have communicated and if you are communicating effectively.

Remember that communication is a two-way street. If you keep the lines of communication open, you will be more aware of opportunities to have a positive impact on players. Fostering two-way communication does not mean that players are free to be disrespectful toward you in word or action. Rather, it is an open invitation for players to express their concerns with the assurance that they will be heard by you.

Try to view your team as individuals and to respond accordingly. For example, a youngster who has low self-confidence may be devastated (or very positively affected) by something that would have no impact whatever on a youngster with high self-esteem. Be sensitive to the individual needs of your players, and you will be a more effective coach.

Timing is important. You can communicate most effectively when the child is receptive. For example, you may find that one player responds much better to instruction if you wait awhile after a mistake, whereas another player may respond best to immediate corrections.

A Word About Parents

Coaching would be so much easier if everything that went on involved only me and the kids. Sometimes I feel that parents forget that this program is run for the kids. They are often more of a problem than the kids. I don't need nine assistant coaches.

A youth sport coach

As we've noted throughout the book, parents can indeed create headaches for the coach. Some of them seem to have a greater stake in what's going on than their children do. Although you may sometimes wish that they would simply stay home, many parents will want to have varying degrees of involvement in the program. You may find it possible in some cases to channel their genuine concerns and good intentions in ways that support what you're trying to accomplish.

Sometimes you will see parents put excessive pressure on the children who play for you. All parents identify with their children to some extent and thus want them to do well. But for some parents this identification process goes too far, and the child literally becomes an extension of themselves. When this happens parents begin to define their own self-worth in terms of how successful their child is. They become winners or losers through their children. The child must succeed or the parent's own self-image is threatened. For these parents, much more is at stake than just a game.

What can you do as a coach to counteract this? It may be important to communicate openly to some parents that by placing excessive pressure on the kids, they can detract from the potential that youth sports can have for enjoyment and personal growth. If you get other parents to understand and reinforce this approach, you can benefit both the player and the parent.

Some coaches have found it useful to meet with parents before the season to discuss this issue. If you can get the parents working as part of a team trying to achieve a common goal, you can reduce the chances that misunderstandings will result in problems. Here are some topics that could be covered at such a meeting:

1. Your appreciation of their interest and concern
2. The goals of the program
3. The specific approach you plan to use. (A description of the positive approach and why you favor it may actually teach the parents some useful principles that they can apply in relating to their children)
4. How they as parents can assist the attainment of the program's goals
5. Your willingness to discuss with them any problems that might arise

Sometimes parents will disagree with what you're doing. Perhaps they won't like the fact that you seem incapable of recognizing the latent superstar abilities of their child. Or maybe they know the *right* way of teaching how to catch fly balls. The main thing is not to get defensive. Listen to what they have to say even if you don't agree. You can afford to at least do this while recognizing that *you* are the coach and have the final say. You may find some of the suggestions useful. But also remember that no coach can please everyone, and no one can ask any more of you than that you be the best coach you can be.

Increasing Self-Awareness and Compliance with the Coaching Guidelines

An important aspect of self-awareness involves insight into how we behave and come across to others — or knowing what we do and how others perceive what we do. One of the striking findings from our research was that coaches had very limited awareness of how frequently they behaved in various ways. The players' perceptions of their coaches' behaviors were actually more accurate than the self-ratings made by the coaches. Successful implementation of coaching guidelines requires an attempt to increase the coach's awareness of what he or she is doing as well as the coach's motivation to comply with the behavioral guidelines.

What are some ways to increase self-awareness? First, to obtain feedback coaches can work together, sharing descriptions of each other's behaviors. They can then discuss alternate ways of dealing with difficult situations and players and prepare themselves for dealing with similar situations in the future. Obviously, this requires an open relationship between coaches, a willingness to exchange feedback that may not always be positive, and a sincere desire to improve the ways in which they relate to children. Other feedback procedures include obtaining input from the players themselves or from a league committee designed to watch and evaluate coaches.

Second, after practices and games coaches should take some time to evaluate their behaviors and actions. When going through this self-analysis, coaches should ask themselves questions about what they did relative to the suggested behaviors in the guidelines. When we observe and record our own behaviors, this is called self-monitoring. To assist in this procedure, a brief coach self-report form is given here.

A Brief Form for Self-Monitoring Desirable Coaching Behaviors

Complete this form as soon as possible after a practice or game. Not only think about what you did, but also consider the kinds of situations in which the actions occurred and the kinds of players who were involved.

1. Approximately what percentage of the times they occurred did you respond to good plays with reinforcement? _____

2. Approximately what percentage of the times they occurred did you respond to mistakes/errors with each of the following communications? (Sum of A plus B should not exceed 100 percent.)
   A. Encouragement only _____
   B. Corrective instruction given in an encouraging manner _____

3. About how many times did you reinforce players for effort, for complying with team rules, for encouraging teammates, for showing team spirit, and so on? _____

4. How well did your team play tonight? (Check one.)

___	___	___	___	___
Very poorly	**Not very well**	**Neutral**	**Quite well**	**Very well**

5. How positive an experience *for the kids* was this practice/game?

___	___	___	___	___
Very negative	**Somewhat negative**	**Neutral**	**Somewhat positive**	**Very positive**

6. How positive an experience *for you* was this practice/game?

___	___	___	___	___
Very negative	**Somewhat negative**	**Neutral**	**Somewhat positive**	**Very positive**

7. Is there anything you might do differently if you had a chance to coach this practice/game again? (If so, briefly explain.)

Behavioral Guidelines
for Youth Sport Coaches

Reactions to Player Behaviors and Game Situations

1. Good plays

Do   Reinforce. Do so immediately. Let the players know that you appreciate and value their efforts, and reinforce effort as much as you do results. Look for positive things, reinforce them, and you'll see them increase. Remember, whether the kids show it or not, the positive things you say and do stick with them.

Don't   Take their efforts for granted.

2. Mistakes, screw-ups, boneheaded plays, and all the things the pros seldom do

Do   Encourage immediately after mistakes. That's when the kid needs encouragement most. Also, give corrective instruction on how to do it right, but always do so in an encouraging manner. Do this by emphasizing not the bad things that just happened but the good things that will happen if the kid follows your instruction (the *why* of it). This will make the player positively self-motivated to correct the mistakes rather than negatively motivated to avoid failure and your disapproval.

Don't   Punish when things are going wrong. Punishment isn't just yelling at kids; it can be tone of voice, action, any indication of disapproval. Kids respond much better to a positive approach. Fear of failure is reduced if you work to reduce fear of punishment.

3. Misbehaviors, lack of attention

Do   Maintain order by establishing clear expectations. Emphasize that during a game all members of the team are part of the game, even those on the bench. Use reinforcement to strengthen team participation. In other words, try to prevent misbehaviors by using the positive approach to strengthen their opposites.

Don't   Get into the position of having to constantly nag or threaten the kids in order to prevent chaos. Don't be a drill sergeant. If a kid refuses to cooperate, quietly remove him from the bench for a period of time. Don't use physical measures, such as running laps.

The idea here is that if you establish clear behavioral guidelines early and work to build team spirit in achieving them, you can avoid having to repeatedly keep control. Remember, kids want clear guidelines and expectations, but they don't want to be regimented. Try to achieve a healthy balance.

Getting Positive Things to Happen

Do   Give instruction. Establish your role as a teacher. Try to structure participation as a learning experience in which you're going to help the kids develop their abilities. Always give instruction in a positive fashion. Satisfy your players' desire to become the best athletes they can be. Give instruction in a clear, concise manner and, if possible, demonstrate how to do it.

Do   Give encouragement. Encourage effort, don't demand results. Use it selectively so that it is meaningful. Be supportive without acting like a cheerleader.

Do   Concentrate on the game. Be "in the game" with the players. Set a good example for team unity.

Don't Give either instruction or encouragement in a sarcastic or degrading manner. Make a point, then leave it. Don't let "encouragement" become irritating to the players.

A Final Word to the Coach-Parent

As a coach you are giving a great deal of time and energy to provide a worthwhile life experience for children. By putting to use the basic principles we have described, you can increase the positive impact you have on young people's lives. Don't underestimate your importance in the personal and athletic growth of your players or the extent to which your efforts are appreciated. Strive to make the experience as much fun and as personally meaningful for the average and low-ability player as for the superstar. You will have a lot of fun in the process.

11

Special Concerns of the High School Athlete

Drugs, College Recruiting, and Other Issues

Not long ago a colleague, a former All-America football player, sat in the stands with his elderly father, watching his son play in a state championship football game. In the middle of the third quarter the son took the ball and ran through the opposition eighty-two yards for what was to be the winning touchdown. As the shouting and cheering died, the grandfather turned to his son, the former All-America player, and proclaimed, "You have now had your greatest experience in sport." Having watched his son perform similar sport heroics a generation previously, the grandfather knew whereof he spoke.

It is obviously gratifying to watch our sons and daughters perform well. They will not all win championship games; many won't make the starting team, but we hope that most school districts will provide an opportunity for all to participate. Sport participation at this age is fun and provides opportunities for self-confidence, acceptance by peers and adults, and fitness.

If sports are all that good at this age, then what are the problems? Many of the issues discussed in previous chapters apply in a special way to high school–aged athletes. We explore a few in this chapter in the hope that we may help make high school sports just a little bit better.

High School Sports: Something Old, Something New

Organized-sport programs for the high school student have been around for about as long as there have been high schools, and countless numbers of students have benefited from them. An example of the great benefit that can be derived from sport participation has been described by the famous American author James A. Michener. He writes the following in his book *Sports in America:*

If there ever was an American boy who was saved by sport it was I. Gardy [his high school basketball coach] was helpful in getting me an athletic scholarship to Swarthmore, so that even my future education depended on sports.

But there was something more. In Uncle George's small gym and in Coach Gardy's larger court we won championships and I came to regard myself as a champion. I carried myself a little taller, worked a little harder in school, built a confidence that was crucial. I drew away from the boys who were headed for reform school and patterned myself after those who were headed for college . . .

I was able to lift myself onto a level of existence I could not have otherwise attained.

Those benefits described by Michener are still received by many high school athletes today. But there is also much that is new and different about sport programs for today's generation of high school athletes. There are a lot more of them participating in many more sports. More than thirty-five different sports are played at the high school level by males. No longer is the sports program limited to football in the fall, basketball in the winter, and baseball or track and field in the spring. In addition to these traditional sports there are several so-called minor sports, such as soccer, tennis, swimming, water polo, and volleyball. Not every young man has to decide between an intense commitment to the varsity football program or no high school sport experience at all. Almost every young man can find a program that suits his interests and talents. He can experience the benefits of a team sport while exploring other academic and extracurricular experiences as well. This has been one of the most gratifying developments in scholastic sports programming in most school districts during the past decade.

The newest athletes on the high school scene, of course, are the young women who have a program of interscholastic sports for the first time. There are some twenty-seven sports approved for high school women. No longer relegated to the pep or cheerleading squads, girls now have their own sports programs, which are rapidly approaching parity with the boys' programs. In many high schools well over half the young women students are going out for some sport and experiencing the same benefits as their male counterparts.

Not only are there more young men and women participating in high school sports, there are also differences in the physical characteristics of today's high school athletes compared with athletes of their parents' day. Today's athletes are bigger and more mature, making it possible for them to achieve higher levels of proficiency and greater intensity in their performances. It is impressive indeed to watch well-coached present-day high school football or basketball teams. One has the distinct feeling that they would be highly competitive with the best college teams of only a few decades ago. Both male and female high school athletes today are taller, heavier, and stronger, and have more endurance than athletes of their parents' generation had. They can run faster, jump higher, throw farther, and hit harder. Not only do they have a greater physical potential for highly sophisticated levels of performance in sports, but athletes today more frequently make an intense commitment to training and practice.

Today's high school sport programs and athletes create new concerns, responsibilities, and demands that many communities, school districts, and parents are all too slow to recognize and deal with. The new breed of high school athletes, competing intensely for higher stakes, needs more sophisticated coaching for peak proficiency as well as safety. As mentioned, the expansion of the high school sport program has created demands for increased numbers of coaches. These demands are sometimes met by assigning coaching responsibilities to teachers with minimal expertise in sport and no professional preparation in coaching, physical education, or sport safety; these teachers may be not even qualified teachers but only interested former athletes from the community. The new scholastic athletes deserve better. School districts and states must demand some level of certification for coaches at the scholastic level.

The larger, stronger, more intensely competitive high school athlete obviously has greater potential for more frequent and severe sport injuries. Two-hundred-pound high school football players and six-foot-tall women basketball players are capable of causing very significant injury to themselves and to others in the sport. In addition to providing adequate coaching, schools must now give serious attention to facilities, playing areas, and equipment. Nowhere in sport is there more need to prevent injuries than in today's high school sport programs. Athletes need the best conditioning programs, protective equipment that is fitted properly and used correctly, and proper recognition and management of their injuries. A recent statewide study of football injuries found that 50 percent of injured players were reinjured when they played again. The inadequately treated and rehabilitated player, returned to play by the well-intentioned but inadequately trained coach, can be at high risk to reinjury. Today's high school athletes are at as much risk to sport injuries as the collegiate athletes of a generation ago, when it was generally accepted that athletes needed professional sports medicine facilities and care. In the expanded sport programs of today's high schools, there is increasing justification for certified athletic trainers and physicians.

Constructive parental involvement is also essential in this new day of high school sport participation. When the student plays a sport, he or she should be able to expect an appropriate degree of support, encouragement, and interest from parents, who should be sensitive to how important sports are to the young athlete. In addition to their responsibilities at home, parents must recognize and accept some community responsibilities if their young people are to have a safe and varied sport experience. Parents must help school boards, city councils, and other civic groups to recognize the important contribution sports can make to the physical and personal development of adolescents. These groups must know that parents in the community want safe facilities, the best protective equipment, certified coaches, and well-planned sports medicine for the athletes. Parents must not accept administrative steps to restrict or curtail sport opportunities. They must support school levies and fees when these become necessary to meet the financial goals of good sport programs in the school. Finally, they must understand that the dollars required to meet these needs are dollars well spent in contributing to the development of today's generation of young people.

The Young Woman Athlete in High School

The high school female in sport is a relatively new phenomenon. Competing in a physical, demanding activity for the first time, the young woman with little sport experience may encounter problems in knowing when to press ahead, when to go all out, and when to take it a bit easy. She may have no understanding of how important it is to pace herself during early workouts and practices. Few things can take the joy out of sport more effectively than overexertion when one is not properly conditioned for an all-out effort.

A high school female athlete should start a conditioning program with her friends before the season begins. She should be ready for that day when the coach suggests some intense efforts to see "who really wants to be on the team." An earlier chapter outlined essential elements of a preseason conditioning program. Starting six to eight weeks before the season to do some stretching, strengthening, and aerobic conditioning exercises with a small group of peers can be fun. It will assure them all a better chance of keeping up when they do turn out for the team.

Even in self-directed preseason exercise, the new athlete may have to be reminded not to exercise when she has pain and, if some joint or tendon area begins to hurt, to ease up and give it some rest. Don't let the young woman believe that playing through pain is a smart part of sport. When it hurts you, you're hurting it!

As parents you should be prepared for the time when your athlete daughter begins to take her sport experience seriously. Women's sports in high school are rapidly beginning to provide opportunities of the same degree of intensity and commitment as have been available to young men. There are also the same potential problems. Academic, extracurricular, and social activities should not be forgotten or shunned.

The day has arrived for young women in high school sports when a superstar can emerge, attracting all the attention and adulation that have come to select male athletes in the past. With all of this can come some exciting days for the parents and some very real responsibilities. If your household is blessed with a young woman high school superstar, be sure her sport activity doesn't unduly rule your household and everyone in it. Learn about the college recruiting process before it starts and get an unbiased appraisal by a respected college coach as to just how much potential your young athlete has in the world of collegiate women sports. Most importantly, keep a close eye on those report cards and take advantage of opportunities to introduce some interest into the family life other than sport.

Supporting Disengagement from Intense Involvement

Prior to high school, athletics for some girls has meant an intense involvement in gymnastics, figure skating, synchronized swimming, or swim racing. The preadolescent and early-adolescent girl willingly accepts the discipline and demanding training programs of these sports because she enjoys the gratifying attention of coaches and parents. As she reaches high school age, her social horizons suddenly broaden and the young man across the aisle in homeroom isn't quite the irritation he was a year ago. Life begins to provide interesting alternatives to five or six hours a day in the gym or at the swimming pool. The young woman athlete may quite suddenly begin to underperform and put on ten pounds of fat that she can't seem to lose.

Painful as it is to accept, it is probably the end of the line. Your Olympic hopeful has had enough. Regardless of the thousands of dollars spent on lessons, fees, medical bills, and trips to competitions over the years, Mom and Dad will do well to prepare themselves to accept some new accomplishments and enjoyments of their young athlete. These talented girls who have been heavily committed to and quite successful in the sports commonly practiced by preadolescent girls often are quite disinterested in team sports in high school. They may have had enough of gyms, swimming pools, and coaches, and perhaps they find it a bit dull to play with less-talented, "average" high school athletes. A recent study of adult women who had been elite competitive swimmers as young girls found that after they left their very demanding swim programs, they shunned active sports and as adults were much less active than women who had never made a serious commitment to competitive sports as young girls. As more and more sport opportunities become available to females in the family, it becomes increasingly important for parents to always be certain that the door leading out of intense sport involvement can be easily opened by a young athlete who has had enough.

The Early and Late Maturer

A large number of the disappointments and problems that surround sport participation at the high school level relate to the involvement in sports by young men who are maturing at a pace that differs from the average. The implications of these maturation differences were discussed in detail in Chapter 3 and present very real concerns in men's sports, where the ability to compete is often related to size, strength, and the levels of physical maturity. Because of the special relevance of this issue to high school youngsters, the major points bear repeating here.

The early-maturing male who has experienced rapid growth in height in the sixth or seventh grade, is shaving occasionally as he starts high school, and is well-muscled before he leaves junior high school has probably enjoyed outstanding athletic success in youth sport programs and on junior high school teams. He has been a year or two more advanced than his teammates who are of the same chronologic age. During high school his teammates begin to catch up in maturation and most will soon attain greater height and size. No longer stronger or bigger than most of his peers, he must face what will be a painful and difficult adjustment to a less stellar role in sports. He had been a star performer because of his early physical maturity and not because of any unique skill or talent. This young man can be directed to sport participation where size and strength are not major determinants of sport proficiency, and he can be encouraged to become involved in some rewarding activities outside of sport participation.

Preventing these high school disappointments that can be distressful for parent and athlete alike may be accomplished during the junior high school years by arranging sport competition with individuals of the same maturing status rather than limiting participation to those of the same chronologic age. The outstanding eighth-grade basketball forward might work out with the high school junior varsity and thus keep his true athletic talent potential in realistic perspective. The early-maturing fourteen-year-old tennis champion should play some matches with the sixteen-year-olds to help her understand whether or not she'll continue to excel.

Frustration and disappointment of another kind is in store for the slow, delayed maturer, the young man whose growth and physical development occur after the rest of his classmates are well on their way to being physically grown-up. If the later maturer is small (and many are), he won't be competitive in most sports because of his size. In wrestling, even though matched in competition on a weight basis, the small late maturer will not do well because of lack of strength and endurance. The small late maturer may find a positive experience in the racket sports or running sports. Even if he is a tall, large, late-maturing boy, he won't have the strength or potential for endurance that will allow him to play up to expectation for someone of his size. Even in sports where strength is not a major determinant of performance, the late maturer will probably have problems due to lack of endurance.

Reassurance is needed by these boys and is best provided by a sensitive physician who can inform the young man and his concerned parents about the normal progression of maturation changes and the individual's timetable for acquiring increased strength and size. If maturation is markedly delayed, an endocrinologist might recommend endocrine treatment to hasten the maturation process.

Drugs and the High School Athlete

A host of drugs are available to high school students on the street and in the school. How does drug abuse relate to newly expanding sport participation by today's student population? Perhaps drug experimentation among those high school students in sport programs is little different from experimentation among the members of the student body in general. However, young men and women who have serious problems with drug abuse are not commonly found in school sports. The young person freaked out on drugs is not going to be very competitive on any sport team.

There are other reasons why the street-drug problem isn't often found in the high school locker room. Participation in a high school athletic program can provide a young man or woman athlete with a very good reason to avoid drug abuse and may give some very practical alternative highs. It puts him or her in an environment where drug abuse isn't, and can't be, "cool." Another reason is that drug use interferes with athletic performance and serious abuse is readily recognized. If a troubled young athlete begins to show some unexplained changes in behavior and a real drug problem is identified, coaches and parents alike must face the issue and, in a nonjudgmental and supportive manner, get the athlete qualified, comprehensive treatment. There are no minor drug problems among high school students.

Although the athlete may be at less risk of abusive use of street drugs, there are a host of sport-related drug abuses that parents, athletes, and coaches must be alert to and be prepared to deal with. In a previous chapter the issue of nutrition supplements was discussed. Vitamin, mineral, amino acid, and protein supplements are all vigorously promoted to the highly motivated population of young athletes. For the healthy young person these materials will have no effect on enhancing athletic performance. As stated earlier, in addition to being useless, they are expensive and potentially dangerous.

Over the years a large number of chemical agents have found their way into sport, supposedly to increase the athletic prowess of the user. It is quite surprising that to date there has not been a single agent among the thousands of chemicals and drugs available that can be demonstrated to increase the athletic performance of a healthy athlete. Currently there are two drugs found in the locker room that present very real dangers. Both have been around long enough to have been studied under rigidly controlled conditions and found to have no significant effect on performance in sport. These are amphetamines ("speed") and anabolic steroids, or male sex hormones.

Amphetamines, although more common on the sport scene a few years ago than today, are still around. They are powerful nervous-system stimulants. They give the athlete an exaggerated sense of performance, reduce powers of perception, alter fine coordination, and increase the risk of injury. The altered, hyped-up, and inappropriate agitation of the amphetamine user usually make the speed freak obvious in the pregame locker room. He or she will need some information and counseling. Further steps may be required if the drugs are being provided by a misguided parent or coach.

Anabolic steroids, synthetic male hormones, are particularly attractive these days to young men in football, the so-called strength sports, and certain field events, such as the shot put and discus throw. The young man trying to increase body weight and muscle mass with a program of increased food intake and weight training will sooner or later encounter some "gym rat" who has hormone capsules or injections that are alleged to really "put on" the muscle. These drugs will increase size and appearance of muscles for a short time if taken in doses that are so large they can't be ethically studied because they are known to be dangerous. This increase in muscle size is of brief duration and is due only to water retention in the muscle. This form of drug abuse is common among competitive body builders.

These substances do not solve the problem of body weight and muscle mass. In fact, they do not increase muscle mass in a healthy young man. Nature has provided him with the ability to produce all of the male hormones he can use.

Anabolic steroids will, in the long run, take their toll. Over time, their presence turns off the production of the male's own hormones and causes shrinkage of the testicles, which produce these hormones. Taking anabolic steroids over a long time can result in scarring of the testicles and permanent sterility. These drugs are not only useless and dangerous but flagrantly unethical. They have no place in sport.

Sickness and Injury

In general, high school athletes are quite healthy. They can, however, encounter minor illnesses brought on by nonspecific respiratory infections, such as colds and flu. To a competitive high school athlete, however, there are no such things as minor illnesses. An athlete with a fever should not practice, work out, or play without a physician's examination and clearance. Fever responses to illness vary a good bit among individuals, but as a general rule, a fever of 100 degrees or greater should put an athlete on the sidelines. Not only will an athlete with a fever play poorly (regardless of all protests to the contrary), he or she will expose other teammates to the infection. There is also a very remote possibility of the cold or flu virus affecting heart muscle so that it won't tolerate the stress of vigorous exercise. Even the finest body can use a little help in combating an infection. That will help make the illness as brief as possible.

On rare occasions the high school–aged athlete can be laid low with something more serious than a common cold or nonspecific viral infection. Infectious mononucleosis or severe streptococcal pharyngitis (strep throat) can put the young athlete in bed for a week or more. Coming back from such a setback can be frustrating and demanding. The athlete will need all the support and understanding he or she can get from parents, teammates, and the coach. As a general rule, it will take at least three days of reconditioning for every day of illness and inactivity. The infection that keeps the basketball starter in bed at home for a week may set him back in conditioning three weeks, after he feels completely well. Getting back to training before he is completely well, free of fever, and able to go to school all day will only prolong his illness and the period of underperformance. Why the body responds in this way isn't well understood, but endurance and strength come back very slowly after a significant infection and enforced inactivity. The experience may be made a bit more tolerable if athletes know how long it is going to take to get back to pre-illness levels of performance.

The increased intensity of competition, the greater strength and size of athletes, and the greater periods of time high school athletes spend at sports all make sport injury a common part of the athlete's life. Elsewhere we have devoted a chapter to the nature and management of sport injuries. Parents should become familiar with that chapter and should share with their athletes information about how the athlete's minor injuries are to be managed at home. (There must be some very good reason for the high school athlete's common complaint that no one could know less about how to manage injuries than parents!) Together you should prepare an optimum treatment plan for minor sprains, strains, and contusions. Know how to effectively provide ICE treatment over the weekend to those hurts from a Friday night game. Have elastic bandages wet and refrigerated and plastic produce bags ready for crushed ice. Know how to elevate a bed to keep an injured ankle from swelling overnight. Have ice cups in your refrigerator to provide ice massage for minor overuse injuries that can be effectively treated during an evening.

Inadequately rehabilitated sport injuries are found throughout high school sports. Adequate rehabilitation of an injured ankle, knee, or shoulder is the greatest unmet need in the medical care of high school athletes, although it is handled by trainers in collegiate and professional sport programs. A weakened leg or arm puts an athlete at increased risk to another injury and obviously hurts performance. Following an injury, an arm or leg should be exercised until the strength and range of motion of joints are equal to those of the uninjured arm or leg. This degree of rehabilitation should be reached before the athlete attempts to return to practice or competition. Getting the athlete to the rehabilitation facility, providing specific exercise needs at home, and observing your youngster's progress are important contributions by parents to injury management.

An additional aspect of injury management, and one that may seem somewhat peripheral to the injury, is the maintenance of fitness during the period of recovery from a sport injury. In addition to the obvious need to stay fit for the most prompt and effective return to competition, the high school athlete needs some sport-related activity to occupy those hours that were previously given to athletic endeavors. The young man or woman with an injured arm can run and do lower-extremity weight training. The individual with a lower-extremity injury can soon begin to swim or work on upper-body weight training. Separating a previously busy high school student two or more hours every afternoon from friends still involved with the team is an invitation to some less-than-desirable activities. Coaches, busy with their teams, cannot be expected to fill these hours. Encouragement and support from home will often be needed.

How to Handle College Recruiting

Soon after the turn of the century, when an Ivy League university constructed a stadium that would seat tens of thousands of spectators for the university's football games, collegiate sports became big business. They have continued to be so. If your son or daughter has had a truly outstanding high school sport career, he or she is going to be invited into this multibillion-dollar enterprise. He or she will be recruited.

For the high school athlete and his or her parents, recruiting can be a very positive culmination of a fine high school athletic career. Or it can mean weeks of irritation, frustration, and anxiety, leading eventually to a much-regretted decision about the athlete's future education and athletic opportunity.

Playing the recruiting game demands a well-thought-out game plan. What follows are some guidelines to how the recruiting game is played and how to end up a winner.

- Know the rules. You had better not play this game *without* knowing them.

- Know how good your athlete really is. How badly are people really going to want him or her in their program?

- Set down some guidelines and rules for dealing with recruiting in your own personal family situation. What are you going to allow and what is going to be off limits in your particular situation?

- Know as specifically as possible what your son or daughter really wants in a school. What kind of an academic program and school should it be, and where should it be located? What kind of sport program will your child be happiest in? These things should be well thought through before the recruiters are in the living room.

- Parents and athletes alike have to realize at the outset that they must be completely honest with themselves and the schools' representatives. Prolonging the attention and the courting may be a titillating game, but the athlete will end up the loser. Recruiters who are not dealt with in a reasonably straightforward way won't be misled. Your athlete isn't the first one they ever tried to entice to their school.

How Will Colleges and Universities Know About Your High School Athlete?

Intercollegiate sport is an intensely competitive activity, and one can feel quite confident that little of the talent that makes for winners is ever going to be overlooked. In spite of the instances in which eventual sport stars were overlooked (Bill Russell was recruited by only one school, and that one very near his hometown), true athletic talent at the high school level is not very apt to be bypassed. High school coaches get great satisfaction in bringing to the attention of college coaches their "well-coached" young stars. The college coaches, their assistants, former athletes, and other alumni all monitor high school sports in various geographic areas on the lookout for the potential collegiate performer. In addition to these scouting efforts, there are highly efficient professional scouting services subscribed to by collegiate sports programs. They provide sophisticated, professional evaluations of high school athletes from all across the country. For an appropriate fee, these services give college coaches professional analyses of high school athletes that they observe in summer camps, preseason workouts, and actual competition wherever an outstanding high school athlete may perform. If your son or daughter has the potential to be a collegiate athlete, college coaches are very apt to know about it.

Provided with the names of potential college athletes, recruiters in college athletic programs commonly send letters to a large number of these good high school athletes in every section of the country to determine, through the athlete's reply, if there is any reciprocal interest in pursuing the recruiting matter further. These mass recruiting letters are intended not to express any commitment on the part of a given school or coach but only to indicate early on whether further interest in a particular athlete is in order. You won't know how interested a school may be in your athlete from that first letter or even subsequent letters. But you will know that to some extent you are going to be involved in the recruiting process and had better take the next step promptly, which is to learn the rules of the game.

Playing any game demands that the players know and abide by rules. It is especially true in this recruiting game. Breaking the rules (and the easiest way to break the rules is not to know them), can cost your son or daughter a college athletic career and perhaps a college education.

The game is complicated and thus the rules aren't all that simple. They are, however, available to parents and athletes in a convenient and understandable booklet provided by the National Collegiate Athletic Association. At the first sign of college athletic recruitment, write for "The NCAA Guide for the College-Bound Student-Athlete" at the National Collegiate Athletic Association, Nall Ave. at 63rd St., P.O. Box 1906, Mission, KS 66201.

The young athlete and his or her parents should be familiar with the information in this pamphlet and should heed the statement on page 6 of the current publication, which states: "Do not permit prospective student athletes to jeopardize their collegiate eligibility through involvement in violation of NCAA legislation."

How Good Is Our Athlete?
How Interested Are Colleges Going to Be?

It is essentially impossible for any of us as parents to be completely objective in appraising the real abilities and talents of our children. It is hoped that most of us perceive our offspring (regardless of intermittent evidence to the contrary) as sensational. But this opinion can lead to a good deal of disappointment and frustration when a family's young athlete enters the recruitment market and a tougher assessment of his or her abilities is required.

The high school coach of your talented son or daughter may also lack objectivity. Yet it is important to get a reasonable measure of the young athlete's true potential and capacity to compete. One suggestion that has served as a good technique for several high school seniors is to seek out a nearby college or junior college coach at a school in which the athlete has no recruitment interest. Make arrangements to get that coach's professional appraisal of the athlete. In this way, at least one major question can be answered: Is the athlete physically big enough and quick enough to play competitively in college? Even the best college coach won't be able to make an athlete significantly bigger or quicker, and these are two traits that will be essential to the athlete's future performance. Most high school competitions don't test these traits to the degree that they will be needed in college competition. The six-foot-five high school basketball player is going to be middle height in college basketball and may be a half-step slow in the eyes of a college coach. It is best to know from the start any limitations your athlete might have and what level of college competition he or she can play at.

Establishing Some Recruiting Ground Rules for You and Your Athlete

Colleges now know about your athlete, maybe some coaches have even seen the athlete in a big game or two, and more letters from more colleges have arrived. What happens next?

Before things go any further, some questions about handling recruiting are in order. Who will talk to the recruiters? How are you to decide whom to talk to? Whom will you allow to visit in your home? How are you to control the effects of these invasions on your athlete's school responsibilities and after-school life? How are you going to keep some balance with other family members' interests and priorities?

If your young athlete has the talent to attract considerable recruiting interest, these questions can present real problems. Some planning can eliminate much of the disruption and potential distress. First, some decisions should be made as to what the athlete sees as top priorities in his college experience.

- How important are prestigious academic opportunities, and in what general academic areas do your athlete's interests lie?
- How competitive is he or she academically?
- Does your athlete need academic assistance?
- Does the athlete feel strongly about staying close to home, or is there a sincere desire to go to some other part of the country?
- Will your athlete go anywhere for the right academic and/or sport program?
- What kind of sport program will the athlete be most successful and satisfied in?
- What style of play, coaching, and team personality will he or she find most satisfying?

Answering these questions early in the recruiting process may eliminate a large percentage of interested schools.

Having thought through these concerns, you must now decide what kind of sport program, academic program, and locations are acceptable. It is not uncommon, if they have kept in close touch with the athlete's high school coach during these discussions, for the family and athlete to have the coach screen all the interested schools and their recruiters. The coach can determine which schools satisfy the criteria developed in earlier discussions. Probably no more than a half-dozen schools will be of real interest to even the most-sought-after high school star. With so many schools to deal with, perhaps you can keep a score sheet, rating each school in various categories as you visit with recruiters and schools and observe their teams and athletes. It can lend some order to what otherwise might be a rather harried experience.

Much of the harassment of outstanding athletes and their families during the recruiting process has been eliminated by present-day NCAA legislation. No recruiting is allowed during the active sport season in high school. The athlete is restricted in the number of colleges he or she can be invited to visit, and the number of visits is also regulated. The number of home contacts is limited to three.

Limiting home visits to three in 1976 led to a system of contact with high school athletes known as the bumper system. Not permitted unlimited visits, college recruiters hired people to learn the life styles and schedules of athletes — when they went to lunch, where they took the bus — and "accidentally" bump into them, dropping a recruiting message. National networks of bumpers have grown, and the intensively recruited high school senior can expect to encounter a bumper. Bumpers are not allowed in schools or athletic areas, or their contacts will count as off-campus recruiter visits.

Visits by recruiters are followed by visits to a limited number of campuses. These visits, of course, are highly structured sales pitches carefully orchestrated to impress the student athlete. He or she will have no problem getting to see that part of university or college life that is thought to appeal most. Students are shown the athletic facilities and they visit with the athletes — perhaps even eat at the training table — but they can spend no more than forty-eight hours at each campus visit.

Experienced coaches often gain a good deal of insight into the personality and maturity of the athlete during the on-campus visit. This social glimpse is an important part of the recruiting process for both parties. Is this big, quick athlete going to be a coachable team player? More than one young athlete has found a school's interest cooled or terminated after the on-campus visit.

The NCAA has just passed new legislation concerning high school academic-performance standards required for admission to varsity athletic programs in member colleges and universities. They are more stringent than in the past and are a sharp reminder to the talented high school athlete not to neglect high school scholastic responsibilities. Recruiters will have little interest in the athlete who has failed to maintain a high school grade-point average well above 2.0.

Thus, during the all-important senior year of high school, especially for the star athlete, when sport performances can be truly outstanding and a heavy responsibility, academic matters cannot be ignored, despite demanding sport and social schedules.

Being Honest, Playing Fair

There are plenty of opportunities in the recruiting process of a talented high school athlete for exploitation of the system — for athletes to abuse the relationship with the recruiting schools and for recruiters to exploit young athletes. Knowing the rules and following them to the letter, knowing what the young athlete wants out of the college experience and pursuing these goals with sincerity, will keep the recruiting experience the reward for good athletic talent that everyone wants it to be. In view of existing regulations, the athlete and family that are hassled by the recruiting process today have no one to blame but themselves. If a family is so privileged as to have a highly-sought-after son or daughter athlete in the house, knowing the rules of the game and playing straight with all parties can make it a very positive and maturing experience.

Sharing Concerns

Comments made by some of today's high school athletes can give us valuable insights into their concerns. Recently, high school athletes from a Midwestern state participated in a series of open forums in which they, their coaches, and parents all had opportunities to talk about high school sports. Strong and widely varied opinions and feelings were expressed by parents, coaches, and student athletes alike. Here are some examples of the comments made:

Coach:

> You ask me if soccer is a matter of life or death? No, it is more important than that!

Parents:

> We question the constitutionality of rules which limit the length of seasons, practices, and training. We feel they are discriminatory, detrimental to the child, and an infringement of individual freedom. In our modern society it is unrealistic for any group to establish limits as to what extent any child may pursue his or her ambitions, and to do so would certainly kill initiative.

> I built a hockey rink in our backyard so my kids could practice every day. I figure I can save twenty thousand dollars in college costs and then they'll have a good shot at the pros.

High school athletes:

> I wish there were rules which would set the amount of time I have to practice every day. I was in the pool at six o'clock this morning and I have to go back tonight and work out again. On Sundays I'm expected to find an open pool and practice all afternoon. Look at me, I'm tired and beat . . . and there's two months left to the high school season and then summer practice starts.

> In every contest someone loses. Athletes can accept that fact. Why can't adults?

> After all, what's wrong with third place?

> The worst part of athletics is having to go home after a game and listen to your dad tell you what you did wrong.

> I don't like a coach that cuts corners to win. One night my coach sent me in to get into a fight with the star player on the other team. We were both removed from the game. Our team only lost me. The other team lost their star. But you know, no one won that game that night.

> When I'm a bench warmer I don't want to be put into the game if it means we look bad.

Don't drop the alcohol rule. Even though lots of athletes violate the rule, those who want to maintain high standards can tell their friends they can't drink because the rule is there.

My parents never missed a game when my brother played hockey, but it took four years to get them to one of my gymnastics meets.

High school athletes did not like parents who

hound you when you lose. I know some kids who have ulcers!

expect me to live up to the reputation of my brother or sister.

still wear their letter jackets.

High school athletes appreciated parents who

don't push me.

still like me even when my team loses.

let me choose any sport that I want to participate in.

took me to lots of games in all sports. I appreciated that.

give me encouragement and understanding. I need that.

Being a parent of a high school athlete can sometimes provide some of your greatest moments. Most certainly it will provide some of the real challenges. Nobody ever said that being a parent of an active growing young person was going to be dull, predictable, or easy. Remember that the goal of sport must always be, first and foremost, to have fun — for the high school participant and certainly for the parent, who can do no better than allow that high school woman or man to continue to grow up and away through experiences in sport.

12

Surviving Youth Sports

*A Commonsense Approach to Some
Knotty Issues*

Prior to beginning this book, we interviewed numerous parents, sport program administrators, coaches, and young athletes. We felt that their input and the kinds of questions and issues that they were grappling with needed to be covered. To give you some idea of the range of concerns that were expressed, here is a sampling of some of the comments we heard as sports medicine and sport psychology professionals:

I am worried about my son. He seems to have gotten things out of perspective as far as sports are concerned. Although he's only thirteen years old, he's convinced that his future lies in college and professional sports. Nothing else seems to matter.

For two years all my son has talked about is playing peewee football. He loves the game and watches the sport all the time on television. This year he finally was old enough to try out for a team. He just got cut and is really hurt. What can I do to cheer him up and show him there is a tomorrow?

I'm coaching a girls' softball team. My players are all average in ability, and some of them have relatively little talent. The problem I'm having is that every time we lose a game, their parents, in order to boost their morale, either blame it on poor coaching by me or on bad calls by the umpires. How can I get these kids to understand reality?

We screwed up and lost the state championship game. I'm so down and out that I'm ashamed to face anyone.

My kids are getting too big for their britches. We're undefeated and the kids are so overconfident that they're getting obnoxious. How can I bring them down to earth?

My son hardly ever gets into games. He likes to play, but he's not very good. It seems like he's going to spend the whole season as a bench warmer. He's talking about quitting. Should I let him or not?

My eldest son has never had much athletic talent. His younger brother is terrific and is really in the limelight. I can see that it's causing problems between them and that the older boy is having trouble dealing with his brother's success. I feel like I need to do something about it.

I went out to watch my son's wrestling practice the other night. I was amazed to see what the coach was doing and saying to those kids. He's a real animal with a foul mouth. I don't want Steve exposed to a coach like that unless he changes. What should I do?

I'm the president of a youth basketball league. We're not having any problems with the kids or coaches, but the parents are another matter. They're yelling at officials and at their own kids, and the games are getting to be a real circus. If things don't get better, we may have to do something drastic.

My husband and I thought that sports would bring the family closer together. Instead, we're chasing all over, and we see less and less of each other. We never do anything as a family anymore, and this has gotten to be a year-round thing. I'm starting to feel that Bob and I are growing farther apart.

Helping Put Athletics in Perspective for Your Child

In the preceding chapters we have shown how athletics can contribute to the personal, social, and physical well-being of youngsters. Sport is an important area in the lives of many youngsters. And for a small number, youth sports are the first phase of a journey that ends in a career in professional athletics. Perhaps you hope that your child is headed in this direction.

To strive for high standards of athletic excellence is commendable. But parents and athletes alike must realize that the chances of actually becoming a professional are remote. Even if your child appears to be a gifted athlete, the odds are overwhelming. The following table shows how selective the process is for football, basketball, and baseball. The figures for football show that only 1 in 6,666 high school football players will go on to play professional football. In basketball the corresponding figure is 1 in 14,000. And for baseball the statistics indicate that only 1 in 1,200 in the free-agent pool actually makes a major league team. Even the small number who rise to the world of professional sports can only count on a very short career. Football and basketball players typically last fewer than five years, and the average career of a major league baseball player is seven years.

Given the reality of the situation, a career in professional sports or even participation at the college level is an unrealistic goal for the majority of young athletes. It is therefore important to impress upon youngsters that sport is but one part of their life. It is all too easy for youngsters and parents alike to harbor fantasies of turning pro and to sacrifice other areas of their development in pursuit of that fabled status and its rewards of fame, money, and glory. It is not at all uncommon for athletes to become one-dimensional. College athletes commonly forsake educational opportunities, to

The Odds Against Becoming a Professional Athlete			
	Football	Basketball	Baseball
High School Seniors	1,000,000	700,000	
College Seniors	41,000	15,000	
Free-Agent Pool			120,000
Pro Draft Picks	320	200	1,200
Pro Teams	150	50	100
Odds	**1 in 6,666**	**1 in 14,000**	**1 in 1,200**

their own later despair. Many of them view college as only preparation for their professional careers in sports. Schoolwork is seen as important only to maintain athletic eligibility. As a result, an alarmingly small percentage of college athletes actually graduate. A study at one Big 10 university found that while the normal graduation rate was 70 percent, fewer than half of the team athletes and only about 60 percent of the individual-sport athletes received degrees. Moreover, only 38 percent of the black athletes had graduated. Another study showed that several western college football powerhouses graduated fewer than 30 percent of their senior football players. Thus, unhappily, the lofty ideal of the scholar-athlete often does not extend beyond the silver-tongued pitch of the college recruiter.

Although the problem may be most evident statistically in college, it doesn't start there. Putting young athletes on pedestals and granting them special favors may in the long run be a disservice to them. Be thankful if your youngster does have athletic ability, but at the same time help him or her to develop into a well-rounded person. As valuable as we believe athletics can be for developing youngsters, we do not believe spiritual enrichment, social and academic development, and quality of family life should suffer. Sports can offer both fun and fulfillment, but there is more to life than sports.

Perhaps the best advice we can give is to encourage your child to participate in sports if he or she wishes to, but at the same time do not allow the tail to wag the dog. Help your child to understand that sport participation is not an end in itself, but a means of achieving various goals. Teach your child to enjoy the process of participation for itself rather than to focus on such end products as victories and trophies. Neither victory nor defeat should be blown out of proportion, and no parent should permit a child to define his or her self-worth purely on the basis of sport performance. By keeping sports in perspective, you can make it a source of personal and family growth.

Providing and Supporting Alternatives

The development of the child as a well-rounded person is best served by participation in a variety of activities. Thus, part of putting sport in perspective involves encouraging and allowing your youngster to grow in a variety of directions, one of which might well be sports participation. But there are two important instances in which sports are not an option in the child's life: One is when a child decides that he or she does not wish to participate; the other occurs when a child is prevented from participating.

In accordance with the "Bill of Rights for Young Athletes" presented in Chapter 1, we support the basic right of every child to participate in athletics. Sometimes, however, children make the decision not to play. When this happens many parents are confused and disappointed, particularly if they have looked forward to their child's involvement in sports. It is hard under these circumstances to respect a child's decision, but in many cases it is very important to do so.

If your child decides not to participate, the most important first step is to find out why. Tell your child that you believe it's an important part of growing up to take responsibility for one's own decisions, but that you wish to understand the reasons why he or she doesn't want to play. You need to find out whether the child's decision is based on a lack of interest in the sport or whether it is based on other considerations. For example, some children would actually like to play but decide not to do so because they don't have confidence in their level of ability or in their acceptance by their teammates. Thus, the most important factor is to decide whether the child would actually like to play. If so, then you as a parent may be able to reassure and encourage your child to give it a try and see how things work out. You should point out to your young athlete that skill levels will increase through participation and that the job of the coach is to help team members become the very best athletes they can.

Sometimes a young athlete decides not to participate because of fear that he or she might let parents down or lose their approval by not performing well enough. If this is the case, you have a golden opportunity to deepen your relationship with your child by exploring his or her feelings and clarifying your own values and expectations. You must face head-on the concern that your child has and the extent to which it is based on reality. The fear may be based on the child's realistic perception of what you expect from him or her. If so, some adjustments in your own thinking may be important. Are you willing to accept your child for what he or she is? Can you love your little bench warmer? Can you be satisfied with your child merely striving to become the best he or she can be, not only in sports but in other activities? If so, and if you can communicate this honestly to your child, this lesson can contribute to lifelong growth.

What to Do If Your Youngster Wants to Quit

At one time or another and for a variety of reasons, most athletes think about quitting. Sometimes a decision to quit comes as a shock to parents, but at other times the warning signs leading up to the decision are very clear.

What are the causes of dropping out of youth sports? In general, the reasons fall into two categories. The first category involves a shift in interests, especially in adolescents. Other involvements, such as a job, a boyfriend or girlfriend, or recreational pursuits may leave little time for sports involvement. In such cases a youngster may simply choose to set other priorities.

The second general set of reasons why youngsters drop out relates to negative sports experiences. Research conducted in the United States and Canada has shown that the following reasons often underlie a decision to drop out:

- Not getting to play
- Undesirable, abusive coaching practices
- An overemphasis on winning that creates stress and reduces fun
- Overorganization, excessive repetition, and regimentation leading to boredom
- Excessive fear of failure, including frustration or failure to achieve personal or team goals
- Mismatching relative to physical size and maturation

If the youngster has decided that other activities are more important, his or her priorities should be respected. However, it is wise to provide a reminder that a commitment has been made to the program and to teammates and that athletes owe it to themselves and to others to honor commitments and to finish out the season. This gives the youngster an opportunity to feel good about himself or herself by fulfilling the obligation through the rest of the season — even if the activity itself is no longer pleasurable.

If the decision to quit is based on one or more of the negative factors listed above, there is a legitimate problem. Again, it is very important that you listen to your child and offer understanding and support. Beyond that, you may discuss some ways to resolve the problems that are affecting the desire to participate. As a last resort you may wish to take some active steps to correct the difficulties. This may involve speaking to the coach or league administrators. In talking with your youngster, you should evaluate how intolerable the situation is to him or her and whether the problems can be worked out. In all but the most severe cases, you can point out that a commitment has been made, and you can encourage your youngster to finish out the season.

If the problems are sufficiently severe, the decision to drop out may be in the best interests of the child. In this case you would want to communicate to your child that although it is important to live up to commitments, you understand that the principle is outweighed by the nature of the problems. If the child does drop out, there may be other opportunities to play in a sports program that doesn't have the negative factors that prompted the decision to quit.

What to Do if Your Child Is Cut from the Team

Heartbreak can be experienced by both child and parent when youngsters are eliminated from sports participation. Surely not all children can be on the team of their choosing, but we believe that every youngster should have a chance to play. Prior to the age of fourteen, the practice of cutting children from sports programs is indefensible. At the high school level it is appropriate to have select leagues to allow gifted athletes to develop their skills. But even at this age, alternative programs should be available for less-talented youngsters who wish to play the sport.

The tragedy of cutting children from sports programs lies in the fact that those cut are almost always the least skilled or those who have discipline problems. It is precisely these children who are in need of an opportunity to grow through sport. Here again, we must choose between a professional model and one devoted to the development of children. Applying the professional model is certain to lead to a lot of disappointed children. As basketball star Bill Russell described the world of professional sports, "Those who don't make the team get tossed out on the street. It is a very serious business." In choosing a program for your youngster, you should keep this in mind.

What should you do if your child is cut from a team? The first thing is to realize that whether or not your child shows it, he or she is likely to feel disappointed, rejected, and perhaps even humiliated. He or she needs your support at this very difficult time. You can give support by acknowledging the disappointment felt by the child. Do not tell the child not to be disappointed or make unrealistic excuses for why it happened. All people must learn to face disappointments in life. You can make this easier if you show that your love and esteem for him or her has not diminished.

In addition to communicating your understanding acceptance to the child and providing reassurance, you can help your child become involved in other programs or other activities. Help your child to investigate options in other programs in the same sport or in other sports. One child who was at first devastated by being cut from a peewee football team was helped by his parents to get involved in a soccer program and is now having a great time. Your child might also choose a nonathletic activity. If so, that decision should be supported.

Being cut is an unhappy experience at any age, but it may be particularly painful at the high school level. Moreover, youngsters in this age range, particularly boys, may be unwilling to openly express the hurt they feel. Creating an atmosphere that will help him explore his feelings may help to ease his sense of rejection.

When Injury Prevents Participation

Being eliminated from a sports program because of an injury may be less painful to an athlete's self-esteem but can in many ways be just as frustrating. For example, a youngster with promising athletic ability can have future hopes dashed by a severe knee or back injury. Here again, parents must try to understand the feelings of frustration, to put up with occasional expressions of this frustration, and to support the youngster through a difficult period. Recognize also that depression, even if not openly expressed, may be reflected in loss of appetite, disturbed sleep patterns, or general apathy. If such symptoms continue or become severe, professional counseling should be pursued.

If a severe injury occurs to your young athlete, it is very important that he or she be seen by a sports medicine specialist. The possibilities of rehabilitation and complete recovery should not be ruled out without consulting an expert in the field. Sports medicine specialists are experienced in dealing with serious sports-related injuries. Most larger communities have specialized sports medicine clinics devoted to diagnosis, treatment, and rehabilitation.

Helping Your Child Interpret Causes of Sport Outcomes

The judgments we make about the causes of events in our lives are of major importance. In understanding something that happens, we are often asked to decide how much the event was caused by us (factors within ourselves) and how much it was caused by factors outside of our control, such as chance or the actions of others. Sports experiences can be an important training ground in forming accurate causal perceptions.

As a parent you can objectively point out what you perceive to be the cause of your child's sport experiences. This can help a youngster form a more realistic way of looking at things. As adults we have our own biases in perception, but we can try to be as objective as possible. For example, if your child blames a loss on a bad call by an umpire or a referee, you might point out that he or she did not play up to capabilities. This helps the child evaluate his or her own role in the outcome. On the other hand, a low-self-esteem youngster who blames himself or herself for a defeat may be helped if you point out that the opponent was highly talented and played well that day.

Some parents are quick to protect or comfort their youngsters by blaming others for losses and failures. It may be the coach, teammates, bad luck, or fate. Their children are never faulted for failure to achieve, for it is always due to some external cause. Parents who express such attributions may be doing their children a disservice by communicating that they are never responsible for what happens to them. Such children may begin to view the causes of what happens to them as beyond their control. As a result they may lose sight of the responsibility they have for their own behavior and its consequences.

When parents do help their children to accurately interpret the causes of events, children can develop a balanced perception of reality. This is but another way that sports can serve as a valuable arena for learning lessons and acquiring skills that can be applied throughout life. As a parent you can participate in and foster the process.

What to Do After a Tough Loss

Children differ a great deal in their reactions to a loss. Some may be barely affected or may forget the loss almost immediately. Others will be virtually devastated by the loss and may be despondent for days.

If your young athlete feels down about a loss, you should give him or her a chance to feel and express the emotion. If, for example, the youngster cries after a loss, this is a realistic expression of depth of feeling and should be accepted as such. At a time like this, a child needs parental support rather than a command to "act like a man."

Respect and acceptance of feeling demands that you not deny or distort what the child is feeling. If your son has struck out three times and made an error that lost the game, he does not want to hear, "You did great." He knows he didn't, and your attempts to comfort him may well come through as a lack of understanding about how he feels. Likewise, it is not very helpful to tell a child that "it doesn't matter." The fact is that at that moment it does matter a great deal.

Is there anything you can do to make your child feel better without distorting reality? One thing you can do is to point out something that was achieved during the contest. A wrestling match may have been lost, but some good takedowns and escapes may have been executed. By emphasizing these accomplishments, you can keep your child from painting a totally negative picture.

Another thing that you can do is to look to the future rather than dwell on the loss. Nothing can be done about the loss, so the most productive view is to focus on what has been learned and can be used again.

Above all, don't blame or get angry with the child. He or she feels bad enough already. Support and understanding, sincerely given, will be very helpful at this time.

Perhaps your young athlete plays on a team that loses regularly. If winning is the only goal that is set, your child will be constantly frustrated. If, on the other hand, scaled-down goals are developed, a sense of accomplishment can result as improvement occurs. Knowledgeable coaches often use individual and team goal-setting to create a kind of game within the game. For example, the team objective may be to reduce the number of errors, strikeouts, fumbles, or penalties in the next few games. Even if games are lost, children can experience a sense of accomplishment as they attain modified goals.

You can promote similar goal-setting on an individual level with your child. In addition to performance goals, you can place emphasis on such important ingredients to success as effort and teamwork. Many a team and many an athlete have been helped to feel as if progress was made toward a larger objective when they succeeded at smaller subgoals.

How to Deal with a Winning Streak

Strangely enough, winning can create its own problems. One is overconfidence and the well-known swelled head. Unless carefully handled, winning teams can become abusive to teams they defeat. And a long winning streak can provide pressures of its own when the emphasis becomes the outcome rather than the process of competition.

When a win occurs the most natural thing is to enjoy it. Youngsters should be allowed to feel good about winning — they've earned it. But they should also be reminded to show consideration for their opponents. Emphasize that it never feels good to lose and that there is no justification for rubbing it in. Instead, tell youngsters to be gracious winners and to give their opponents a pat on the back or a handshake in a sincere manner.

During a winning streak, most athletes experience not only the pleasure of winning but also the increased pressure not to lose. An additional danger is that if a team wins too regularly and too easily, they may get bored and take their success for granted. A focus on effort and continued improvement can provide an additional and meaningful goal for youngsters. It is important to communicate that you expect continual striving for victory. Again, winning is to be sought, but it is not the only objective. Finally, don't allow your youngster to rest on past laurels. Point out that past success does not constitute a guarantee of no mistakes or losses in the future.

Parental Behavior at Practices and Games

In Miami directors of a youth baseball program found it necessary to move games to midafternoon and to prohibit parents from attending them because of repeated unruly behavior on the part of spectators, including profanity and the physical assault of an umpire.

Near Hilo, Hawaii, a dispute among the parents of rival peewee football teams spilled over into a full-scale riot after the game. A group of parents from one town later invaded the enemy community with lead pipes and baseball bats, inflicting severe damage and injury.

In Talequah, Oklahoma, a district judge ordered a youth baseball player's mother to stand trial for murder after she fatally shot another player's aunt at a baseball game. The mother, a special-education teacher, shot the other woman after the aunt made derogatory remarks about her son's playing ability.

In parts of New York City, high school basketball games are played in locked gyms with no spectators to protect players and officials from violence.

Major league baseball team manager Billy Martin, himself a veteran of numerous baseball brawls, expressed strong feelings about the behavior of some parents at youth sport games. Martin said, "I've watched games where little kids were trying to play while parents were screaming from the stands, 'Show some guts.' That made me sick. It's not fun for little kids to play the game under pressure like that."

Much of the joy of being a youth sport parent comes from watching your child practice and compete in games and meets. Most children also appreciate their parents' interest and attendance. What youngster isn't bolstered by looking up into the stands and seeing Mom and Dad in rapt attention?

It is most unfortunate when incidents such as those described above occur. Fortunately, the vast majority of parents behave appropriately at youth sport events. But the minority who misbehave can spoil it for all the rest. It takes only a few inconsiderate parents to turn what should be a pleasant atmosphere into one that is stressful for all concerned.

Program directors, game officials, and the participants themselves have a right to demand that spectators observe certain standards of behavior. Two prominent sport scientists, Rainer Martens of the University of Illinois and Vern Seefeldt of Michigan State University, suggest the following minimum guidelines:

- Parents should remain seated in the spectator area during the contest.

- Parents should not yell instructions or criticisms to the children.

- Parents should make no derogatory comments to players, parents of the opposing team, officials, or league administrators.

- Parents should not interfere with their children's coach. They must be willing to relinquish the responsibility for their child to the coach for the period of the contest.

Although they may appear totally engrossed in the game, many children are very sensitive to what is being said from the stands. Laughing or poking fun at a player who makes a mistake may inject some humor for the spectators, but it may be heartbreaking for the child. Likewise, "bench jockeying," or attempts to rattle the opposition, is inappropriate at the youth sport level. Indeed, one can question whether such actions are in good taste at any level.

A Little Boy

*He stands at the plate with his heart pounding fast; the bases are
loaded; the die has been cast.*
Mom and dad cannot help him, he stands all alone.
A hit at this moment would send the winning run home.
*The ball nears the plate, he swings, but he misses; there's a groan
from the crowd with boos and some hisses.*
A thoughtless voice shouts, "Strike out, you bum"
Tears fill his eyes; the game's no longer fun.
Remember, he's just a little boy who stands all alone.
*So open your heart and give him a break, for it's moments like
this a man you can make.*
Keep this in mind when you hear someone shout;
Remember, he's still a little boy and not a man yet.

Anonymous

It is easy to get caught up in the action of the game and to
suddenly find yourself verbally participating. Parents should never
shout criticism or instruction at their children. This applies also to
teammates and opponents. If you wish to shout encouragement or
praise, make sure that your positive approach extends to the other
players as well. But again, codes of sportsmanship dictate that
recognition be given to opponents as well. There is no reason why a
great play or a great effort made by the opposition should not also
be appreciated.

Children are not the only ones who are the targets of barbed
comments. Some onlookers seem to forget that youth sport
programs could not exist without volunteer coaches and officials
who give unselfishly of their time and energy. They deserve your
respect and support, and they should be treated with dignity. As
tempting as it may be, it is simply not appropriate to second-guess,
yell instructions, or disagree with decisions made by the coach.

It is as American as apple pie to boo and criticize judgments
made by officials. But such behavior has no place at the youth sport
level. Officials are human and they make mistakes. Like your child,
they are amateurs. The officials are honestly trying to do their best.
Booing their decisions will not change the outcome or improve the
situation in any way. Moreover, parents who "get on" officials
provide very poor models for their children, and such behavior can
prove highly embarrassing to the young athlete.

Good sportsmanship among spectators is a goal worth working for. We believe that it is the job of parents not only to keep tabs on their own behavior, but also to remind others, if necessary. Coaches and league officials have a big enough job without having to police spectators. The rule of thumb for all spectators is that nothing in their actions should interfere with any child's enjoyment of the sport.

Getting Along with Your Child's Coach

Some of the knottiest problems that arise in youth sports involve the relationship between parents and coaches. Any time another significant adult enters your child's world, it may require an adjustment on your part. First of all, as we mentioned in Chapter 1, you must be willing to put up with another potential hero. You must also be willing to give up some control and influence in an important area of your youngster's life. Taking a back seat to another adult even temporarily isn't always easy. But things can get even more complicated and challenging if you find yourself at odds with coaching decisions that affect your young athlete.

Your responsibility for what happens to your child does not cease when he or she enters a sport program or joins a team. As a parent you have every right to be involved in and to look out for your child's welfare. The tricky part comes in deciding how and to what extent it is appropriate for you to be involved. When does appropriate concern become interfering and meddling? At what point must your understandable concern with the happiness and well-being of your child be tempered by respect and understanding for the role of the coach? What should you do if issues like the following crop up?

- Your child isn't getting to play enough during games.
- Your child is not playing the position best suited to his or her talents.
- The coach is mistreating youngsters either verbally or physically.
- The coach is engaging in inappropriate behavior, such as bad language or hazing of officials or opponents.
- The coach is using technically incorrect, questionable, or possibly dangerous coaching methods.

- The coach is demanding too much time or commitment from the youngsters, such that the sport is interfering with other activities.

- The coach is losing perspective of the purpose of youth sports and seems preoccupied with winning, thus putting additional stress on players.

Because each situation is somewhat unique, there are no cut-and-dried answers that apply to every case. Nonetheless, there are some general principles that can be helpful in approaching and resolving such problems.

When incidents such as those listed above occur, it would be a mistake not to consider them problems. Perhaps the best starting point is to view them as problems that you and the coach must work together to resolve. The key to doing so is establishing communication and then keeping the lines of exchange open.

Many parents first become aware of problems when their children complain about the coach. If this happens, the first step is to sit down with your youngster and discuss the problem to get his or her point of view. You should listen and express concern, but do not form a judgment or make condemning statements about the coach. After listening, you may decide that the issue does not warrant your involvement and that it might best be worked out by your youngster and the coach. You can help your child by giving suggestions on how to approach the coach and express concerns. If you can help resolve the issue without your direct involvement, your child may learn some very important interpersonal skills and gain confidence in his or her problem-solving ability.

If the situation seems to warrant it, you should contact the coach and indicate that you would like to have a conference. Such discussions should never occur during practices or games and should not include the child. Having your child there may put the coach on the defensive and create an adversary relationship between you and the coach. What is needed is a mutual problem-solving approach.

When you meet with the coach, you can help create a positive atmosphere for exchange by telling the coach that you appreciate his or her interest in the children and contributions to the program. You might also communicate that you understand how demanding the role of a coach is. In other words, try to create an open and receptive atmosphere for discussion.

Next, indicate that there is an issue that you would like to discuss with the coach and that if there is a problem, you would like to work with the coach in resolving it. Here are some examples of ways in which you can introduce the problem:

Jason told me that he would like to get to play more during games. He feels that since he comes to every practice and tries hard, he'd like to get to play more. (*Note that the coach is not being directly accused of not playing Jason enough, which might create defensiveness. Whenever possible, frame the problem in terms of a positive goal to be achieved.*)

I have been to several of your basketball practices, and I have seen the drill where you have the children practice taking charging fouls and being run over by an offensive player. I am concerned about the possibility of injury. Is there some safer drill that could be substituted?

I've seen some of the kids get very upset after being yelled at, and I am concerned. I wonder if there isn't some way of making it more fun for the kids. Sometimes we adults don't realize how easy it can be to hurt feelings.

Sara joined the program because she wanted to have fun and because she enjoys playing softball. There seems to be such an emphasis on winning and so much pressure put on the girls to perform that at least for Sara, it's becoming stressful rather than constructive.

After expressing your concern, you might once again acknowledge what a difficult job coaching is, but that you thought the coach would want to hear about your concern because you believe he or she has the best interests of the children at heart. Then tell the coach that you would like to hear his or her view of the situation. Again, the emphasis should be on resolving the problem together.

Communication is a two-way street. You will need to be prepared to listen honestly and openly to the coach's point of view. For example, his opinion of your child's ability and deserved playing time may be somewhat different from your own. And the role of coach requires that he or she make a judgment about playing time.

Parents who voice their concerns are often surprised when they are asked to participate in a solution to the problem. For example, one father who disagreed with the coach's way of teaching a particular skill was asked by the coach to assume the position of assistant coach. The coach acknowledged that he had little experience in that particular area and that he would appreciate the father's assistance. In another instance a mother who expressed concern that her son was not playing enough was asked by the coach to practice with the son so that he would improve enough to play more. Thus, we must sometimes be prepared to contribute time and effort as well as opinion.

In some cases you may find that it isn't possible to correct the situation with the coach. If you feel strongly enough about the issue and are convinced that the coach's actions affect the physical or psychological well-being of the children, you may need to take further action. Several options are available. First, you may appeal to a higher authority. If a coach is being abusive to children, for example, this should be brought to the attention of league administrators. If the issue concerns only your child and not others, the solution may be to request a transfer to another team and coach. The last, most drastic, and least desirable alternative may be to remove your child from the program. This should always be a last resort, because it may have some negative consequences of its own. For example, the child may be called a quitter.

Fortunately, most coaches are firmly committed to providing the best possible experiences for youngsters. When approached properly, they will usually be open to parents' concerns and motivated to deal effectively with problems.

Up to now, we have been focusing on undesirable things that might come to your attention. But relating to your child's coach goes beyond this. When things are going well, it is important to offer your support, encouragement, and appreciation to the coach. This adult is playing an important role in your child's life. All too often, the only feedback coaches get from parents is negative. It is important to let them know when they are doing a good job. They deserve it.

Giving Attention to the Nonathlete in the Family

Children who are heavily involved or gifted in athletics have no problem in getting lots of attention. In some families so much attention is paid to the star athlete that brothers and sisters may fade into the background. This is most likely to happen when parents are heavily invested in sports themselves and prize athletic accomplishments. It is important to keep in mind that all children need attention, love, and support from parents. When nonathletes feel pushed into the background, parents may find themselves having to deal with jealousy, feelings of rejection, and lowered self-esteem.

Although involvement in sports is to be encouraged and valued, other areas of achievement should be given equal billing. Find something special in each of your children to love and celebrate. The nonathletic brother who is trying hard in school or who is musically inclined or has a knack for making friends deserves recognition and support just as the young athlete does. Try to impress on your children that each of them has unique gifts and endearing qualities and that you are aware of them. Also emphasize that growing up involves finding out which things children are best at and enjoy most. Approval of each child as an individual lays the foundation for self-acceptance in all of your children.

Your involvement with your young athlete may vary in degree, but it will almost certainly require a time commitment on your part. This should not detract from personal time with the nonathletic children in your family. We frequently suggest to parents that they keep a daily record of the amount of time spent with each of their children over a two-week period. They are often surprised to find that a huge amount of time is spent on the activities of the young athlete. If you find this to be the case in your family, you may wish to block special time around the activities and interests of your other children. When this is done, no child in the family will feel left out.

Helping Your Marriage Survive Youth Sports

Youth sports can be an important element in family growth and solidarity. Anytime parents share significant experiences with their children, they can help build stronger family ties. Stronger bonds can be forged not only between the parents and children but also between the parents themselves. The sports environment is a place where you and your spouse can witness and enjoy the growth and development of your child. You cannot sit in a classroom and watch academic skills blossom. But you can have a sideline seat to the development of your child's athletic and social skills. Take advantage of the opportunity.

As you are well aware, having children can place certain strains on marriage. The coming of a child into your relationship means increased demands on time and effort. Children are very needy, and your attention and devotion are the foundation of good parenting. Each phase through which a child develops places different stresses and requirements on you and your spouse. As a result parents find that they have less time for themselves and for their spouses. Just as youth sports can be a double-edged sword to the athlete, so it can affect husband-wife relationships in a positive or negative fashion. Couples need to be aware of this fact and to be prepared to counteract the potential pitfalls.

Children not only are a blessing but also offer special challenges to a marriage. Many couples center their lives on children and are unaware that their relationship is remaining static or perhaps even crumbling from lack of attention. Many couples unwittingly drift apart during the child-rearing years only to find at the midlife crisis that they have little left in common except their children. Couples who before marriage dreamed only of spending their lives together now find that they have become married singles. They become absorbed in their day-to-day activities and come to discover that the excitement of their earlier years together has died. On the surface all appears tranquil. The serenity comes from a lack of awareness of what is missing in the relationship. The escalating divorce rate and the number of single-parent families provide grim evidence of this.

Your entry into a youth sport program can free up more time for you and your spouse, or it can place even greater demands on your marriage. As parents discover, there can be an increased time commitment to such things as driving children to and from practices and games, serving on parent committees, or acting as coaches. Some parents find to their dismay that practices are held during the dinner hour and that their kitchen becomes a cafeteria with several shifts. The fun and togetherness of family meals become a thing of the past. For most families this is only a seasonal phenomenon. But for others whose youngsters have year-round involvements, this becomes the normal pattern of living.

Families whose children are in elite individual sports, such as gymnastics, swimming, or figure skating, often bear an extremely heavy responsibility. One mother whose daughter is an up-and-coming figure skater rises each morning at three to take her daughter to the rink for practice. This family spends up to $20,000 per year on lessons, ice time, travel to meets, and equipment. Because of these time and financial commitments, the family has not had a vacation in five years.

To the extent that a sports program does detract from family togetherness, it is important to have family time to make up for time spent apart. When a child is involved in games and practices several nights a week, parents should make it a point to spend Saturday and/or Sunday together as a family.

For some couples youth sports become a deceptive blessing. Such couples avoid facing problems in their marriage through youth sport involvement. The focus of their lives becomes the child in the athletic arena, and they become so wrapped up in his or her activities that they avoid dealing with marital discord.

Perhaps the most important thing is to decide exactly what your priorities are and what you want out of the sport experience, not only for your child but also for the rest of the family. If your priorities are to grow closer as a family, then you need to think of ways in which you can use sports to improve and not damage this process. For example, are you willing to put up with the chaotic family-dinner schedule that often results? Some parents have answered this question with a firm no and have allowed their children to participate in only those programs that do not interfere with the routines of family life. In most instances, however, you will have to balance the negative against the positive things that your child and the family might experience in a sports program. Be aware of what is likely to be required and how much time and effort you are willing to devote. Once into a program, you should also keep in mind that you can easily be seduced into more and more involvement. You will have to take your turn in car-pooling and you may be asked to perform other duties.

Special challenges arise for husbands and wives when there is a great difference in interest and involvement in sports. For example, if Mom is totally uninterested in baseball and Dad is a baseball fanatic, there is the chance that Dad will get more and more heavily involved while Mom becomes a sports widow.

What do couples do, then, to compensate for the demands that youth sports can make on their relationship? It is important that parents give time to their own relationship just as they give time to their children. Private moments spent away from the children can serve to maintain and invigorate your relationship. Recreational pursuits for you and your spouse, an occasional weekend away by yourselves, dinners out, and a cultivation of interests you share in common can help maintain the sparkle in your marriage.

Marital bliss doesn't just happen automatically; it comes from actively working at it. All couples must continue to find ways to improve communication. Get into the habit of talking regularly about your thoughts and, especially, your feelings. As long as the lines of exchange are kept open and problems openly discussed, your relationship with your loved ones can not only endure, but deepen.

Index